MARIA JOSÉ DA COSTA OLIVEIRA

The New Public Relations:

Communication between private and civic sector

1ˢᵗ Edition

GlobalSouth
P R E S S

For more information, please contact info@globalsouthpress.com
or go to http://www.globalsouthpress.com/

Book design by **Héctor Guzmán**

Editing and revising by **Marisol Alvarenga**

The New Public Relations:
Communication between private and civic sector

Includes bibliographical references and index.

ISBN:

978-1-943350-12-4

1. Organizational Communication
2. Public Communication
3. Democracy
4. Deliberation

GlobalSouth
P R E S S

Editorial Board:

For all those who believe and act or have the prospect in values such as social justice, human rights, global perspective and future generations, because they will understand how much communication plays an essential role for society.

DEDICATION

This book is the result of the study that I conducted in my postdoctoral developed at ECA / USP under the attentive and dedicated guidance of Professor. Dra. Heloiza Matos, who I am proud to have been advised in my doctoral and post-doctoral research projects, and also honors me with the preface to this book.

There are many reasons that cause us to move forward, to grow, to dream, and in my case, they are all linked to people. People who have influenced me and that are influenced by me, people who bring their values, their perceptions, their opinions. For this is that it is so important to recognize the value of relationships we have established because they transform us and at the same time, make our convictions more solid.

So I thank to those with who I share, as is the case of my beautiful family (Celso, Marilia, Giovana, Juliana), my mother (D. Dora), my siblings, my siblings in-law, mother in-law, and nephews, my uncles, my cousins ; my friends, my colleagues, my teachers, my students, and some more.

This book, that addresses the importance of communication, actually is the means to express how relations between people are so essential to our existence that can not be, in any way neglected.

Thank you to all of you.

FOREWORD

Imagine a society where barriers between the social sectors become permeable: the first sector (the State) would adulterate the second and third sectors (the market and civil society), and vice versa. As a result, the mass media and social networks as fourth sector would fill the spaces of debate and mutual influence with other sectors. And to complete the process of interaction, universities as producers of knowledge and fifth sector, would include the agents and beneficiaries of knowledge, covering the most diverse social strata. In addition to this scenario, there is the transition of a representative to a participatory system, endowed with a progressive appreciation of the individual and collective human being . Here is where the topics covered by Maria José da Costa Oliveira's book are inserted.

In this imaginary world to the experience of citizens, corporations become involved in assignments previously restricted to the State, civil society, the media and universities - without losing, however, its market perspective. Since this is possible, it is now a challenge of research and theories in various fronts of human knowledge. And this same process is repeated for each of the aforementioned sectors, which would inherit characteristics that before were unaware to them. This cross-pollination would imply, however, on some possibilities and perplexities. For example, the greater or lesser distinction between public and private; the institutional and personnel; statal and non-governmental; the corporate and societal; advertising, marketing and public communication; lobbying and political communication; etc.

The book by Maria José da Costa Oliveira effectively discusses the effects of this cross-pollination of corporations, in a perspective from above all conveyable . Thus, the author comparatively analyzes the degree of public sensitivity (first sector), social (third sector), communication (fourth sector) and education (fifth sector) of the corporations positioned in the second sector. In other words, the author seems to be interested in the convergence between the stockholders and stakeholders in a context of broad participation and debate in the defense of common interest. All this in a scenario where social sectors do not overlap with their own individuals, and whose legal entity ends up acting as individuals - as sentient beings, endowed with ethics and conscience, and as responsible and active citizens in their community of daily and political experiences and talks.

Under this transgenic context, the pursuit of profit gains new dimensions. If traditionally the primary goal was to remunerate shareholders (stockholders), corporations are now demanded by society to defend the interests of all stakeholders (inside and outside the company and the market). This implies open consultation, communication and adaptation channels of processes and behaviors in all timeframes (short, medium and long term). To take on new functions, organizations are becoming more informed and sensitive to the movements of citizens in social networks, with the common good, more involved in counterbalance the State failures, most dedicated to informing and communicating, and more likely to invest in technical and civic education.

To the extent that corporations are humanized, in the aforementioned convergence between legal entity and individual, they also acquire positions of citizen: wishing to express themselves, discuss, influence, deliberate on issues involving the national and international community. Therefore, organizations tend to include the ideal of citizenship, in and out of his frames: they incite engagement and participation in the public and private businesses, and also in public causes - such as sustainability. They can also take parliamentary forum features: treat the stakeholders as civic agents that interact and discuss the direction of corporate policies. In other words, stimulate parliamentary civil activities. But this participatory openness may indicate in a critical sense, a kind of interference in the corporate direction and market.

On the other side, the communication process between organizations and their audiences may choose to focus on institutional policies that have potential repercussions in the media, the criteria of profit and institutional visibility in the market. In this case, public customers/consumers of these organizations end up being turned down, for not being aware of the real actions of these social policies - as analyzed by the author. In this case, the sustainability projects awarded by Exame magazine and Aberje, as the strength of the disclosure, are concentrated among market peers.

By ignoring the benefits of these actions, both in everyday conversations and in the media, but especially in social networks, customers turn into reviewers of the quality of services of the organization - as can be seen in the results of the empirical research presented in this work. Here is a key point of Maria José da Costa Oliveira's book: amid such miscegenation of sectors, agents, interests and objectives, she aims to analyze the benefits of these sustainability policies, highlighting the participation and reciprocity indicators in groups and between civically engaged citizens respectively - always aligning them to the pure concepts of public communication and social capital.

Given this, one might ask what would be the future of such pure concepts in corporations that behave as citizens and are structured as parliamentary forums? And at the same time, they use appeals that attract media attention, society, and the actual and potential customers. Whatever the answers are, in this case the communication is the first relief.

With or without adjectives, communication is strategic and stands as the set of processes that enables (the existence of) all social sectors, and their interaction. As well realized by the author, only the correct scientific approach to communication phenomenon will bring some light to this fascinating new world before us. Maria José da Costa Oliveira goes strong in this debate by proposing that organizational communication can and should take on a new face, promoting concrete actions in the field of democracy and citizenship, involving the market and the actors who are the targets of public communication. Do you want to participate in this dialogue? So be sure to read this book!

Profa. Dra. Heloiza Matos

PhD do Programa de Pós Graduação da Eca /Usp

Heloiza Matos e Nobre

PART I

1.Introduction

This book aims to analyze the interactions, convergences and conflicts between the notions and organizational and public communication practices in Brazil. Based on the literature, it will target concepts and methods, as well as empirical research to assess their applications, identifying joints and impacts between these concepts.

Assuming that technological advances have contributed to the transformation of the citizen's profile as new subject able to influence organizational and / or public policy, it is included study of cases of companies that have been awarded for their environmental responsibility projects.

It is also carried out analysis of the ways in which are held informal communicative interactions of private organizations for social networking. After all, changes in civic engagement standards of citizens are calling for the strategies and organizational communication policies take into account the demands of the prevailing public spheres and their contribution to the creation of social capital.

In the current social, political and economic environment, the private organizations are inserted into the public sphere, being impacted and generating impact in the other constituent elements of such sphere, which could be governmental organizations, civil society organizations, groups advocating different interests and even at the initiative of individuals / subjects.

In this sense, one can glimpse the importance of this analysis, which aims to identify the essence of organizational communication policies, leading researchers and practitioners to reflect on their possible entanglement with public communication.

Therefore, this book is to analyze the possible overlaps between organizational and public communication, considering the articulation ways and limitations of the concepts in practice.

It is important to identify whether the scenario consisting in the democratic process advances, new technologies and citizenship has brought effective impact on organizational communication policies, to the point of requiring greater entanglement with the concept of public communication, allowing a new perception in the way organizations design their communication policies.

Another question that arises is whether the organizational communication, in the current context, demand integration with public communication in order to establish a global communication policy, which intertwine the interests of the organizations with those of society. Such entanglement can be exemplified by means of social and environmental responsibility actions that reveal the public face where the companies operate.

The research object consists of the organizational communication policies and environmental responsibility, developed by companies that have had their projects recognized by awards, such as the prizes Exame Sustainability Guide and Aberje, trying to identify the interface of explicit policies in public communication.

Some hypotheses guide the development of research and the structure of the chapters. The first hypothesis considers that when the organizational communication is part of the public communication as a key concept, tends to align both, the interests of the market and the state. This would require an initial approach to the concept of public communication, understood as a foundation for analysis .

Another guideline hypothesis for this book is the serious consideration that in a democratic society, in which the organizational communication includes public communication as a fundamental concept of the public sphere, there is the tendency to give recognition of *stakeholders,* professional communication and society. This assumption leads to the need to examine the interaction between organizational and public communication, which is made in detail in Chapter I. However, as the case also highlights the democratic framework, Chapter II plays an instructive role in this regard .

The third hypothesis states that organizational communication policies can contribute to public communication, by means of developing within the private sphere, social and environmental responsibility initiatives, which are also reflected in the public sphere. However, the relations between private and public might tend to blur in front of the influences a sphere exerts on the other. This hypothesis stimulated the development of the second section of the chapter, which I devoted to approach the communication in corporate social responsibility actions intertwining private and public.

The fourth hypothesis asserts that those companies adopting integrated organizational communication policies will have no restrictions in market results. Therefore, they are those that generate positive impact in the public sphere, since they posses strategic and comprehensive view of their commitment to the issues of public interest aspects analyzed in Chapter I and III.

The last hypothesis bets that the actions that stimulate manifestation,

debate and interaction among organizations and social groups have influenced the business communication policies, social institutions and public bodies. This would definitely show the links between organizational and public communication, permeating the analysis of all the chapters.

Thus, from a theoretical point of view, this book will present referential authors that analyze the public sphere concepts and democracy, participation and deliberation. In this way and from a critical perspective, it will allow to focus on the interface between organizational and public communication.

Empirical research, highlighted in Part II, elucidates the behavior in communication practices of organizations, interactions between private and public. It also draws the actions aimed concerned to environmental responsibility, enabling analysis of the level of this relationship from a restricted approach to a sample of Brazilian companies´courses of action. Even though with limitations, this panorama will allow a better understanding of the challenges that present themselves to the effective range of the interaction between public and organizational communication practices.

Therefore, It is expected to examine the overlaps between public and private, from the entanglements and conflicts established between public communication to the organizational communication ways and limitations; as well as the analysis of the impact of the public communication as a guiding principle of the organizational communication . However, it is important to mention that these concepts are articulated in practice.

From a theoretical point of view, it shows up possible convergences and / or conflicts between the concepts; from the empirical point of view, it is analyzed the perspective that the interaction between public and organizational communication remains a challenge.

CHAPTER I

1. Connections between public communication and organizational communication

This chapter initiates with the concept of public communication, central to this work, precisely because it represents a new perception of communication policy in democratic contexts. It also states its commitment to citizenship and promotes dialogue with society and the public interest.

Brandão (2007) emphasizes that this communication should be performed by all who are part of the public area. Within a democratic context all sectors, institutions and individuals integrate their different roles to form different public spheres in society.

Matos (2007) analyzes that public communication raises plurality of styles, genres, views, opinions, worldviews. And this plurality highlights the importance of dialogue, debates, discussions and deliberations that lead to decision-making in situations that impact society. He also tells us that public communication supposes reception of demands by channels and messages from multiple poles, either from the State to the society, from the market to the State and society to the market.

For Duarte (2007, p. 59), public communication centers the process on the citizen, while Matos (2007, p. 47) endorses it as plural space for national debate intervention on the issues of public interest.

It is Interesting to include the contribution of Haswani (2011, p. 82) in the present analysis, which highlights that public communication comprises various processes and makes not only public but also private actors interact ; he also has a view to enable the relationship between the state and citizens, in order to promote a process of social and civil growth.

From this perspective, Haswani distinguishes between public communications carried out by public subjects, and that carried out by private law subjects either by duty or voluntarism, respectively.

There is no doubt the State has the duty to act for the public good. In the meantime, the private sector having adopted policies of social responsibility / sustainability, reinforces how much its actions and processed communication within the organizational orbit can contribute to the public interest. There will be discussion towards this topic in the following chapters.

Rosso and Silvestrin (2013) conclude that public communication is the hope to expand democracy, making the citizen responsible in matters of public interest and individuals able to impact life in society.

The authors (2013) emphasize public communication as a practice of social responsibility of public organizations, which also paves the way for the present analysis. They understand this role to private organizations, once it is independent of the involved actors nature. Public communication has the commitment to prioritize the public interest in relation to individual or corporate interest, being held in public spaces and on topics of public interest.

Thus in the democratic context, there is no way to limit public communication from the State's actions as it preferably involves joint and integrated actions, and initiative of various sectors of society, of course giving priority to the public interest.

Therefore, the need to analyze the role of organizational communication in this public perspective arises: substantial advances have been recorded in research and publications in recent years; they have been addressing the concepts of both organizational communication and public communication . Researchers and authors have engaged the issues, showing a considerable advance in studies concerning these concepts.

However, these concepts tend to be built in parallelly, and their approaches have been restricted indicating the overlapping of organizational and public communication. These concepts do not intersect, as one follows the trail of the private sphere, the other relates to the public sphere.

In the current social, political and economic scenario there is no way to perform the analysis of organizational communication in isolation, not taking into account their impact and amalgam with the public sphere.

As Kunsch indicates (2009, p.75) on organizational communication:

> "Today, it can be said that studies are more comprehensive and include many issues in a broader perspective, as discourse analysis, decision making, power, organizational learning, technology, leadership, organizational identity, globalization and organization, among others ."

Acknowledgments as expressed by Kunsch suggest that further studies start to contribute to expand the analysis on the communication role in society.

It is interesting to observe the concept of organizational communication evolution, which was previously referred and adopted: "the American communication thinking, (that) in a traditional perspective was focused on realizing the organizational communication mostly on the internal environment and the information management processes." (Kunsch, 2009, p.75)

In a historical overview, this author also shows how organizational communication concept has evolved. Before "the focus was on administrative / internal communication and information management processes, in communication networks, in the channels, messages, culture and organizational climate; in the organizational structure and flows, networks, etc ; the inputs and outputs of organizations "(Kunsch, 2009, p. 75).

However, different approaches have come to reveal new possibilities. Kunsch (2009, p. 75) when citing George Cheney and Lars Thoger Christensen (2001, p. 235) notes that the authors draw attention to the interdependence and interrelations of internal communication with the outside.

As a result, it seems possible to perform analyzes that help to advance the relationship between the micro and the macro environment, between the individual and the citizen, between the individual and the collective, between the private and the public, and finally, between organizational communication and public communication.

Haswani (2011, p. 93) also endorses this view when analyzing the recent studies of organizational communication link, an opening perspective to dialogue and joint participation with other sectors.

Habermas (1997, p. 30) summarizes in the following quote, the importance of participation, the joints, the discussions in the public interest, that indicate the role communication plays in the process.

> "The fact that the citizen is also responsible for the State co-management has implications that go beyond the sphere of political relations in that strengthen the fabric of links between the citizens themselves and place in discussions of the agenda issues which, although originating in private sphere, interfere with the community's way of life."

The need of organizational communication policies is evident to be aimed to the public interest, thus establishing the interface with the public communication, as can be exemplified by corporate social responsibility actions.

At the same time, when it comes to organizational communication one can not ignore the concept for coverage, since there are different types of organizations. According to Corella (. 2006, p 43), they are private corporations, micro, small and medium enterprises, public institutions and nonprofit organizations.

However, for analytical purposes this book will focus on organizational communication of private companies (whether small, medium or large) that aim to profit and which apparently can prove as opposed to the public interest.

Companies are also already responsible of their impacts to society and the environment, and they will require the adoption of practices and policies on social and environmental responsibility.

Then assessment needs to highlight the importance of companies social performance, and the intertwining role of both public and private communication come to play in this context.

2. Corporate Social Responsibility (CRS) intertwining private and public

Various communicative resources and the changes in civic engagement standards of citizens are demanding that organizational communication strategies and policies take the demands of society into account .

Such demands are increasing and becoming complex; they also can no longer be restricted to the state. Thus, companies participation of the third sector and the civil society is fundamental.

López (2011, p. 65) makes a note that clarifies the relationship of the companies with public interest matters, by indicating for example that public communication moves in different scales or levels. All this responds to the interlocutors, the operation intention or the way, which will possibly cover at least five communication dimensions: policy, media, the State, the organization -which is the emphasis of this book- and social life.

In addressing the organizational dimension, López (2011, p. 65) rightly endorse a central aspect of the approach of this book. Contrary to the assumption that "public" only concerns to the State, it is understood that a private organization is a scenario in which messages and interest groups circulate to dominate and impose their senses; it is clear there is an inner unique "public sphere" .

The author completes its analysis by highlighting that the public of an organization is the set of its members, marked by understanding, imaginary, codes of behavior, practices, benefits and instances of collective interest. Thus, the author also considers it possible to speak of public communication in a corporation or a private company. (2011, p. 66)

However, if here I advocate for the importance of organizational communication aligned with public communication, we need to understand to what extent the initiatives of companies in their social responsibility actions are defined based on the manifestations of the social groups to which they relate.

Of course, it is worth to reinforce that such definition requires an organizational communication policy that understands social groups and individuals as interlocutor subjects, citizens who are aware of their needs and want organizations -whether public or private- effectively contribute to society; not only for their self-promotion or ensuring image gains, reputation and brand, but to bring real benefits to everyone.

This view is reinforced by Rolando (2011, p. 26) when he considers the public communication not only as the manipulation of power, but mainly as the territory in which many subjects (even if confronting) seek legitimate interests, and use information and communication not so much to sell something, but to present their identity, vision and goals.

The author (2011, p. 27) addresses the classification of what he calls public utility communication, citing different profiles, including the company's communication, when it gives more to the conditions representation for development and growth , making it an area where all these subjects act and interact in the context of general interests.

However, the author considers there is still reluctance toward this company's communication profile as fully admissible in the context of public utility communication.

This perception, which excludes companies communication focused on public utility, is related to a reduced vision. The author describes how frequent is the absence of dialogue spaces between the institutions and their audiences.

Matos (2011, p. 44) particularly refers to public institutions and even mentions the manipulative character of some communication actions of certain political institutions. However, this absence of dialogue spaces can be seen very often in communication policies of all types of organizations, especially private enterprises.

This author also reinforces the guiding idea of public communication concept citing Noble (2011), who advocates to necessarily include (all) social actors that make up the public sphere to debate and formulate proposals for action or policies that benefit (all) society.

There are companies' initiatives that seem to follow such guidance, establishing channels of communication for internal and external communities, to also manifest about their real needs, even indicating actions that turn into social projects of great impact.

When this occurs, organizational and public communication increasingly tend to weave a context that requires the alignment of the interests of organizations with those of the company. Thus, communication policies should take into account key issues such as ensuring participation of all in the organizational context, and this democratic ideal must go beyond the State sphere.

Some companies not only include concern for the public interest, as they have also set up communication policies for the community to consult and manifest.

However, communication policies aligned with the public interest are dependent on the values with which the organization commit, and which therefore are incorporated into its organizational culture. Therefore, a question that presents itself as fundamental is to understand the level of awareness that companies are able to have dedicated to public interest issues.

So forth, it is useful to mention the model of the Seven Levels of Consciousness developed by Richard Barrett (cited Fejgelman, 2008, p. 154-156) and identify the differences in organizational commitment.

Table 1 - Levels of personal and organizational awareness of Richard Barrett, 1998 *

Levels	Personal Awareness Levels	Organizational Awareness Levels
1	**Survival** - it focuses on the physical survival issues.It includes values such as financial stability, wealth, security, self-discipline and health. The potentially limiting aspects of this level are generated by fears around survival. Greed, control and caution are included as limiting values.	**Finance** - It focuses on the financial issue and organizational growth. It includes values such as profitability, shareholder value, employee health and safety. Potentially limiting values of this level are generated by fear of survival, as control, territoriality, caution and exploitation.
2	**Relationships** - This level is concerned with the quality of interpersonal relationships. It includes values such as communication, family, friendship, conflict resolution and respect. The potentially limiting aspects of this level result from fears about loss of control or consideration. Limiting values include rivalry, intolerance and need to be liked.	**Relationships** - it includes the quality of interpersonal relationships between employees and customers / suppliers and includes values such as open communication, conflict resolution, customer satisfaction, courtesy and respect.The potentially limiting aspects of this level are born of fears related to loss of control and personal consideration. This generates manipulation, guilt and internal competition.

3	**Self-esteem** - It emphasizes the issue of recognition. It includes values such as being the best, ambition, professional growth and reward. The potentially limiting aspects of this level stem from low self-esteem or loss of control. Potentially limiting values include status, arrogance and image.	**Self-esteem** - This level is concerned with management practices that improve the working methods and the delivery of services and products, including values such as productivity, efficiency, professional growth, skills development and quality. The potentially limiting aspects are the result of low self-esteem and loss of control, and it also includes values such as status, arrogance, bureaucracy and complacency.
4	**Transformation** - It focuses on self-realization and personal growth. It contains values such as courage, responsibility and personal development. This is the level at which people work to get rid of their fears. This requires an ongoing questioning of one's beliefs and assumptions. It is also the level at which the professional gets the balance in life.	**Transformation** - Visa continuous renewal and the development of new products and services.It contains values that overlap the potentially limiting values in levels 1-3. At this level, it includes values as liability, employee participation, learning, innovation, teamwork, personal development and knowledge sharing.
5	**Meaning -** It faces the concern of the individual with the search for meaning and community. Those who operate as at this level no longer think in terms of employment or position, but in terms of mission. This also contains values such as commitment, creativity, enthusiasm, humor / joy, excellence, generosity and honesty.	**Internal cohesion** - It focuses on the community spirit within the company. It includes reliable values, integrity, honesty, awareness of values, cooperation, excellence and justice. The result is joy, enthusiasm, passion, commitment and creativity.

6	**Making a difference** - It brings the issue to make a difference in the world.It is also the active involvement of the local community level. Individuals operating at this level honor the institution and the contribution. They may be concerned about the environment or local issues. It contains values such as counseling, community work, empathy and environmental awareness.	**Inclusion** - It focuses on maturing and strengthening relationships and achieving official. Within the organization, it includes values such as leadership development, ability to mentor, ability to be coaching and conducting officially. It externally includes values such as collaboration with customers and suppliers, building partnerships, strategic alliances, community involvement, environmental awareness and making a difference.
7	**Service** - It reflects the highest order of internal and external connection. It focuses on serving others and the planet. Individuals operating at this level deal well with uncertainty. They demonstrate wisdom, compassion and forgiveness. They have a global perspective and are concerned with issues such as social justice, human rights and future generations.	**Unit** -It reflects the highest level of internal and external connection. Within the organization it includes values such as vision, wisdom, ability to forgive and compassion. Externally it includes values such as social justice, human rights, global perspective and future generations.

* (Cited Fejgelman, 2008)

As it can be seen, there is the evolution of the level of consciousness, either at a personal or organizational levels, depending on the culture, values and maturity. This suggests that effectively committed companies with the the public interest are those located at higher levels of consciousness, as the lower levels are restricted to seek personal survival or meet the financial sustainability of organizations.

Such approach leads us to understand the reasons why companies have advanced in the interaction between public and private, while others show far this perception. The society demands from companies its commitment to the public interest, especially those in the first level that refer to performing social / environmental actions. However, they tend to hide the real intentions of their practices, camouflaging basically promotional interests.

In a democratic context, applied to all who are part of society, participation, dialogue, engagement should be based not only on public communication policies, but on organizational communication policies mainly considering the boundary between the public and private tend to blur.

This panorama associated with the evolution of technology having a mark of the advent of social media, strengthens citizenship and puts companies challenged to also act in the public interest, albeit unintentionally, demanding adequate preparation so that they can deal with the positive or negative manifestations that carry either the internal or external context.

Companies and all types of organizations must include in their social and environmental policies communication policies, able to allow the engagement, participation and deliberation, contributing to the creation of positive social capital.

Consequently, communication policies can no longer be limited to the organizational context, expanding its operations and goals for public life. Of course, this conduct requires communication practices not to be just confined to promoting information.

In this sense, communication also incorporates advocacy, which refers to defend a cause, to be the process that requires the civil society actors participation to influence policy decisions at different levels.

When dealing with advocacy as a public communication strategy, López (2011, p. 70) also indicates that business groups rather create non-profit foundations to list the topics of social responsibility.

These are foundations dedicated to advocacy, so organizations do not risk crossing the fine line between the private interest of corporate character, in the public interest. Thus, the author warns that:

> When that line is crossed and the foundations business originated begin to make mobilizations seeking benefits for their owners, end up doing lobbying and probably abusing its image, types of slips that are frank and open corruption (2011, p. 73)

Undoubtedly, Lopez concern is quite appropriate, as there are many actions presented as public interest, but reveal themselves fully geared to particular interest, with losses to society. This can be exemplified by numerous scandals reported in the media that involve companies , government and third sector.

Even so, the boundary strength between public and private tends to blur from the moment it is understood that the public interest must be above private interest.

As previously pointed out, social / environmental responsibility policies appear to represent more explicitly the path for the establishment of the relationship between organizational and public communication. Therefore, the empirical research included survey and analysis of award-winning projects in the Exame Sustainability Guide and ABERJE Prize focusing on social and environmental projects made public, making it possible to identify the companies concerned.

However, before including a survey and analysis of empirical data, we must remember that the concept of relationship between public and private only makes sense when it unveils the democratic scenario. This would reveal the role of communication in this context, not being a mere adjunct with available techniques and tools, but as a central element in the democratic public sphere. Thus, we shall now consider the relationship between democracy and communication, analyzing both the public and the private sphere.

Chapter II

1. Public sphere and private democracy

Numerous approaches about public sphere and democracy have been held. However, here it is essential to rescue the contribution of authors like Habermas (1997, 2003), Esteves (2003), Marques (2008), Gugliano (2004), Santos (2002), Gomes and Maia (2008); they offer the fundamentals to understand the new public spheres issues and consequences, which maked by deep changes began to form in society.

Habermas, one of the main references in studies on public sphere, analyzes that this is located between the state and society, allowing us to understand the origin of the impact that causes organizational communication in public communication and vice versa.

Marques (2008) indicates to ensure everybody's participation in debates and speeches equally in formal and informal contexts, actors should follow procedures to assure the conditions of equal participation and consideration of all.

From this statement, it can be assumed that equal participation with reflection in the public space should be considered in the organizational context; however, Marques quotes the interaction between social actors should be mediated by accountability (accountability), equality, mutual respect and political autonomy. Therefore, communication becomes key tool of information flow between the periphery and the center. (2008)

In turn, Gugliano (2004) highlights the relationship between capitalism and democracy. However, since capitalism favors economic issues and undermines democracy in the citizenship and civil right's context, this symbiosis causes doubts on the ability to generate benefits against the process of physical deterioration, cultural, social and environmental sustainability of the planet.

Gugliano (2004) also shows the prospect of qualitative policy analysis studied by different authors, and points out at the trajectory of new democracies that characterize the third wave of democratization, precisely in the context of citizenship and civil rights.

As can be seen from this his analysis, democracy is one of the key aspects discussed using, on the one hand authors who try to enclose the political regime, and on the other authors who defend its scope to society as a whole.

Democracy delimited to the political regime is restricted to the state sphere, instead of extending it to the economic market and society. This definition takes private organizations not to apply the democratic prerogatives in their management or strategic planning goals, giving predominance of private profit over the welfare interests of the population.

Thus, the separate economic market of democratic management strengthens the barrier between the public and the private, favoring the boundless ambition. Therefore, there are frequent activities related to economic market fleeing ethical and moral standards of contemporary societies.

All these considerations head to rethink the theory of democracy, for as proposed by Santos (2002), widening the democratic canon.

To make progress in the senses of democracy, it is necessary to democratize the non-state sphere (Santos, 2002), to characterize a model that goes beyond the political regime, able to emphasize mediation between the local and the global, which will also incorporate new problems that might interfere with the democratic approach .

Esteves (2003) deals with the historical constitution of public space and its difficulty in becoming truly democratic for the participation of civil society. He also highlights the centrality of communication, especially the mass media in the process of constitution of a public space, currently fragmented and diluted.

While the author states that this space would not have extinguished all its vitality. After all, the same fragmentation that arises as a concern by Esteves, can also be seen as a natural feature of a context that values diversity.

According to him, civil society was reconfigured throughout history, turning the "bourgeois society" into a strong structured social nucleus of autonomous voluntary associations, not only for the State but also in relation with the economy.

With the regenerative power that civil society can insert, a public space depends on the precise demarcation of its borders with the State, and the promotion of responsible social action.

Gomes (2008, p. 39) shows an essential aspect that I have covered in this book , which is that "public reasoning or the public use of reason in discursive situation, always takes place as debate, as discussion. All institutions that endows the public sphere are destined to ensure something like a permanent debate or discussion of private individuals in public. "

The very public sphere is understood, then, as the scope of discussion in society between private individuals. Themes and issues, such as generated outside or within the public sphere, here are submitted to public communication in the positions game and replicas. (Gomes, 2008, p. 39)

In this relationship between public and private sphere, Gomes (2008, p. 39) deepens the analysis on the topic by finding that an audience is not a mere assemblage of individuals, but a meeting of private individuals. This meeting is free, able to present positions discursively, turn them into arguments, and confront the other positions in a protected discussion of non-rational and not argumentative elements.

The role of communication is highlighted in Gomes approach (2008, p. 40), especially when he suggests that an audience is a gathering of individuals , capable of opinion and dialogue. So Gomes makes clear that the public sphere is the scope of argumentative negotiation of citizens, the domain of rational-critical debate, the social dimension of the practices and procedures by which the assembled citizens can design, specify, reject or adopt positions on any matter of common interest.

On the one hand the public sphere is intertwined with the private sphere. Though, according to Gomes(2008, p. 43), there are differences between them: the public sphere, although it occurs in private business spaces, is distinct from the private one . This includes exactly two characteristics: a) the intimate sphere of family, where subjectivities are structured and constituted , being a place of psychological emancipation, and a background on which the sphere of private business stands ; b) the private sphere itself is the life production and reproduction place, the economy, the market.

The author also addresses another crucial aspect here: he reminds that economic activity recognized as private since the Greeks, now has also publicly collective relevance .

However, Gomes (2008, p. 43) points out that the private sphere is assured as such even before the public sphere is requested. In this sense, the author quotes Habermas (1984), for whom the separation between public and private sphere is the competition for private interests, which have been basically left to be regulated by the market and sent out of public contest of opinions.

The same author also considers that the public sphere is not an arena for market relations, but a theater of discursive relations about any objects. The political public sphere, more restricted, materializes in argumentative arenas in which public affairs are considered. (Gomes, 2008, p. 44)

With this approach, we can identify how the notion of public and private was constituted historically, having as basis the understanding of their established relationships. Once again, this confirmed in the words of Gomes (p.54) that the public sphere, little by little, is no longer the social dimension of argumentative exposition of matters related to the common good, but that of media discursive exhibition of private positions that want to assert publicly , and therefore need a plebiscitary consent of the public.

The public and the private sphere, whose binding I tried to evidence, are considered as two overlapping blades by Gomes, because they resound the issues and present voices to the public sphere, and the problems experienced in the private sphere.

Of course, it is not the totality of what is originally lived as private and intimate that flourish on advertising, but only those aspects caused by deficits in functional systems that reach and affect the world of life (Gomes, 2008, p. 100).

Therefore, the role of companies in developing social responsibility policies becomes central, since there are social deficits that drive companies to act in the public context, either by peer pressure (which demands their participation), or by willingness (which ensures their sustainability in a society toward more potential development).

Gomes (2008) reinforces this notion when considering that public, private and intimate spheres touch, since the flow of topics and issues always keep a vector going from private to public.

2. The role of deliberation in organizational and public communication policies

To meet the objectives proposed in this book, an approach about the concept of deliberation is necessary, precisely because it represents the link that weaves democracy and communication. It refers to the action of opinion in order to influence decisions.

Marques (2008, p. 13) considers that the resolution can be understood as a discursive activity able to connect formal and informal communication spheres, in which different actors and speeches establish a dialogue to assess and understand a collective problem or a matter of public interest.

Kim, Wyatt and Katz (2008) define deliberative democracy as a process in which citizens participate voluntarily and freely in discussions on public issues. Noteworthy, that deliberative democracy is also a discursive system where citizens share information about public affairs, political talks, formation of opinions and participation in political processes.

To Gomes (2008), democracy needs the deliberative bodies act as public sphere to protect the common good of the arbitrator domain, not necessarily to give reasons for its decisions.

The deliberative politics plays a crucial role in the democratic process, because according to Habermas (1997, p. 28), it gets its legitimating force of the discursive structure in the formation of opinion and will. This fulfills its social function and appreciates the expectations of their rational quality results. Therefore, the discursive level of public debate is the most important variable.

To characterize the democratic process Habermas cites Cohen through the following postulates:

a) The deliberations are held argumentative way, therefore, through the regulated exchange of information and arguments between the parties, which collect and critically examine proposals;

b) Deliberations are inclusive and public;

c) Decisions are free from external constraints;

d) Deliberations are also free of internal constraints that could endanger the participants level of equality (P.29)

The communicative act is responsible for establishing relationships, stimulating social ties, or according to Habermas, "which links the right partners is, ultimately, the linguistic bond that maintains the cohesion of any communication community." (Habermas, 1997, p. 31)

Communication gains strength in the democratic context, as Habermas states "if we want to tackle issues dealing with the regulation of conflicts or the pursuit of collective goals without employing the alternative of violent conflicts, we must adopt a practice of understanding, whose processes and communicative assumptions, however, are not simply in at our disposal."(1997, p. 36)

For Habermas, "the results of deliberative politics can be understood as a power produced communicatively, which occurs with the potential power of actors who are able to make threats, and the administrative power that lies in the hands of employees." (1997, p. 73)

To Benhabib (cited Maia, 2008, p.165), deliberative conceptions of democracy are based on the principle that "decisions that affect the well-being of a community should be the result of a free and reasonable deliberation procedure between citizens considered equal morally and politically. " He also says that any decision must be understood as argumentative process (p. 166), which needs to be stimulated in discussion forums.

Thus, not only Habermas, but also Cohen and Benhabib highlight how much the communication as argumentative process plays a crucial role in deliberation, and is able to establish links among participants.

In this sense, companies can fulfill an important public role when creating possibilities, for example by promoting interrelations with social groups to participate in forums that they also promote and include public interest issues. Of course, this role has been developed by some civil society organizations, but it can be strengthened by alliances with the private sector.

Other than that, considering the defense statement that democracy is not restricted to the political sphere, it must permeate society as a whole, involving all sectors, and including the private sector. Thus, by encouraging organizational policies to create discussion spaces within companies, the private sector will be consistent with democratic politics.

From this perspective, it is valuable the Maia´s affirmation (p. 180) when she asserts that the public sphere is not only understood as unique and global, but rather constituted by a variety of audiences organized by topics and causes of common interest.

Maia believes that the public deliberation helps to distinguish pragmatically between the particularistic and selfish claims , and those with greater collective appeal (p. 192).

To my proposal to precisely analyze the similarities, interactions and conflicts between organizational communication and public communication, Maia´s approach is very useful, especially as the author emphasizes a policy of expanded conception, attentive to practical contexts of everyday life and to the settings of civil society , and the complex interactions that take place between private and public domains.

Mansbridge (1999, p 211) for example, conceives the deliberation not only between organized audiences- that is to say "between formal and informal representatives in designated public forums, from the conversation between constituents and elected representatives or representatives of groups politically oriented organizations" but between unorganized public - in other words, "the media conversation, the conversation between political activists and everyday conversation in private spaces". (Maia, p. 196)

Marques elucidates the intersections between the communication process and the public debate, noting that the public debate subject presents himself or herself as a key reference in the formation of a public sphere in a broad discussion that can contribute not only to build a democratic system marked by the approach between formal government instances and informal forums for discussion among citizens, but also to better care and appropriate approach to political and social conflicts fought in contemporary societies. (2008, p. 11)

The deliberation can be understood as a discursive activity able to connect formal and informal communication spheres, in which different actors and speeches establish a dialogue that aims at assessing and understanding a collective problem or a question of general interest. (Marques, 2008, p. 13)

Thus, a society that embodies the democratic culture tends to adopt the resolution as a natural process in all public and private instances.

Marques (2008, p. 184) also considers the citizens that have real opportunities to deliberate treat each other not merely as objects but also as subjects who can accept or reject the reasons given by the laws that are binding on each other.

In this sense, communication policies, whether organizational or public, should be based on this new subject of plural democratic society , with space for debate and diversity of opinion.

As already highlighted, the communication in the democratic context requires to consider the relationship between public and private sphere, as from this dynamic it is respectively extracted the interface between public communication and organizational communication.

Habermas alleges that private centers of the world of life are characterized by intimacy, and therefore protected from advertising, as they structure meetings between relatives, friends, acquaintances, etc., and weave the biographies of well-known people. The public sphere maintains a complementary relationship with this private sphere, from which the public holder actually recruited from the public sphere. (Habermas, 1997, p. 86)

Strengthening the analysis, although each sphere maintains its own characteristics, the boundary between public and private tends to be increasingly diluted in a scenario notably marked by technological advances, through the internet and social media, which allow the social relations become increasingly hybrid .

In the relationship between public and private, there is influence from a sphere over another, because as Habermas states:

> Only the spheres of private life have an existential language in which it is possible to balance, at the level of a life story, the problems generated by society. The problems thematized in the political public sphere initially transpire in the social pressure exerted by the suffering that is reflected in the mirror of personal life experiences. And to the extent that these experiences find their expression in the language of religion, art and literature, the literary public sphere, specializing in joint and discovering the world, intertwines with politics. (1997, p. 97)

3. Respect in the deliberation.

Cohen (cited Mansbridge, 2009) lists criteria to legitimize the decision. That is to say: freedom, equality, consideration and consensus. It is not my purpose to analyze each of them, however as these criteria are underpinned by mutual respect, I will try to elaborate some considerations about its importance on deliberations.

If there is no respect from any side involved in debates, there isn´t either a way to strengthen the relationships, or how to encourage the deliberation process because as stated by Mansbridge (cited Steiner), participants must treat each other with mutual respect and equal interest.

Sennett (2004, p. 67) considers respect seems so fundamental to our experience of social relations and self being, that we must define it more clearly. It is necessary to analyze its meaning from some given synonyms: status, prestige, recognition, honor and dignity.

According to this author (2004, p. 71), status refers to the position of a person in the social hierarchy, while "prestige" is understood as the status that raises emotions in others. Even seemingly clear, the relationship between status and prestige, Sennett alerts to its complexity and points out that structurally the character of respect toward the others' needs, the status becomes hardly convenient and the prestige is simply not appropriate somehow.

Referring to the recognition, Sennett (2004, p. 73) mentions Rawls -for whom its meaning is to respect the needs of those that are heterogeneous, and Habermas -who advocates respect to the opinions of those whose interests lead to disagreement. Thus, recognition can help to generate social awareness.

To assign honor, Sennett (2004, p. 73) suggests, first its incorporation as conduct codes, and second as a kind of elimination strategy for borders and social distances. The author uses Bourdieu as reference, pointing at his consideration that states honor supposes an individual who always sees through the eyes of others, which needs the other for their existence, because the image he has of himself is indistinguishable from that presented to him by others . In this sense, the honor also generates social awareness, even at the cost of aggression against strangers.

Finally, dignity is either applied to human dignity, and to labor dignity. Both stands are seen as universal values: the dignity of the body is a value that everyone can share, while the labor dignity can only be achieved by a few. (Sennett, 2004, p. 77)

Therefore, Sennett´s considerations toward respect are barely frequent, and become complex in an unequal society as respect is closely related to others´ recognition.

Even showing this complexity, respect should permeate the organizational communication policies in democratic contexts, contributing to the alignment with the public interest, as well as with the meaning of the resolution. After all, not only in public spheres, but also in private spheres, independent groups or institutions to which they belong, individuals have the right to participation, argumentation, and dialogue.

There must be respect from all sides, such as from the company to the community, from the community to the company, otherwise its absence can cause inhibition of the deliberative , participative, engaging processes.

After all, as Gutmann and Thompson (cited Steiner) mutual respect requires an effort to appreciate the moral force of the position with which we disagree. Although freedom, as already mentioned, is one of the outstanding criteria to the legitimacy of the resolution cited by Cohen, it can be concluded that there are limits to this freedom: the lack of respect can inhibit the expression of potential participants in a deliberation process.

At the same time, respect can not be disassociated from transparency and confidence in order to strengthen social capital, which deserves a special approach to follow.

However, as endorsed by Mansbridge (2009, p. 223), despite the mutual respect to be understood as a fundamental criterion in the deliberation process, it is important to remember that, both in a public forum and in everyday conversation, there is justifiable opportunities for offense, non cooperation and threat of retaliation.

After all, "no one ever listens carefully to others, and members of dominant groups particularly think they do not need to hear the members of subordinate groups. So subordinates sometimes need the motivation of anger "(p. 224), as not always equal, another criteria presented by Cohen is not often guaranteed in the deliberative processes.

As Mansbridge cites (2009, p.224), good deliberation must include what comes before and after, as the conversation of individuals and their positions with people who think similarly or opposite.

Anyway, it can be concluded that in relative freedom and equality environments, considering both reason and emotion, everyday conversation and the formal deliberation should help participants understand their conflicts and affinities. (Mansbridge, 2009 p. 230)

Whether in formal resolution as in everyday conversation, we must judge that a participant transformation as private person to citizen depends on the types of solidarity and commitment to the principles involved. (Mansbridge, 2009, p. 230)

In this sense, even with the natural presence of conflicts, respect stands out in the deliberations and reinforces its role in linking people, leading to the current need to emphasize the concept of social capital.

CHAPTER III

1. Social Capital and communication in public and organizational spaces.

As highlighted earlier, the various communicative resources and the changes in civic engagement standards of citizens are demanding that the strategies and organizational communication policies also take into account the demands of the public sphere and its contribution to the creation of social capital.

The relationship of the concept of social capital with this approach is because, in order to establish relations between public and private, it becomes an essential condition for links establishment between the component members of the organizations. These are ties that help ensure the engagement either in relation to intra-organizational goals, or to the objectives aimed at public interest.

Reis (2003, p. 43) when analyzing Putnam´s work "Making Democracy Work", 1993, considers social capital as a key variable to identify the successful implementation of potential public policies and programs in different contexts.

This consideration helps justify the relevance of social capital as a concept within the analysis that assumes the public and private interface in a democratic deliberative context, indicating that public policies and programs also involve private organizations as society members.

Thus, it is worth remembering that social capital is closely linked to the social and communication networks available to the interactions of social actors (Matos, 2009, p. 101). Matos also highlights that "the social network can be scaled by the confidence that members attribute the participants and the consequences associated with this feeling." (Matos, cited Duarte, 2007, p. 55)

Matos (. 2009, p 37) quotes Coleman, for whom the capital can be found in two types of structure: in social networks running in an enclosed space (a club, association or union, with its own rules and sanctions) or in a social organization or institution with a specific purpose (business, government, cultural association, political party, NGOs). In the latter case, the organization or institution can move away from its primary goal (profit, management, election) to integrate a social action or cause.

This definition can be considered the central point that justifies the proposed analysis of the concept of social capital in this book,since it suggests why it is often possible to witness private companies breaking their organizational boundaries to also exercise a public role.

Matos (2009, p. 38) analyzes that Coleman in the education field, and Putnam in civic participation and behavior of the institutions are sources of inspiration for most of the studies of social capital.

These latest studies focus, according to Matos (2009, p. 38) in nine fields: family; juvenile behavior, schooling and education; virtual civic and community life; work and organization; democracy and quality of government; collective action; public health and the environment; crime and violence; and economic development.

Considering these fields, it is possible to perceive that studies on social capital have already emphasized the organizational universe, including private companies and, in that sense, Reis (2003, p. 44) also weaves considerations based on Putnam (1997, p. 177), for whom social capital is seen as a voluntary and decisive facilitator of cooperation in the establishment of virtuous circles that favor the good institutional performance.

Reis (2003, p. 45) examines the role of social capital in various organizations, including for-profit, using as reference Dietlind Thomas Stolle and Rochon (2001) who seeks to specify the theory of social capital more precisely when the impacts of different types of affiliation impact on the development of public social capital.

However, the author warns the presumption of Stolle and Rochon is, for example, to orient associations on profit activities which will be less prone to feed community ties of reciprocity in comparison to schoolar protection associations or public parks in a given location.

Although this observation is useful and it can't be avoided. I emphasize that it is not here to deepen the comparison between social capital in organizations that aim to profit from those that do not.

Clearly, different approaches by authors who are dedicated to the topic result from the concept of social capital. However, I focus my analysis on the social capital at the organizational level.

Vale et al (2006, p. 46) consider that social capital is manifested through social networks that make cooperation and collective action for mutual benefit possible , within organizations, groups and communities.

The authors consider that there is a shortage of analysis on the role of social capital in organizational studies. Due to this, they bring an important contribution when demonstrate the organizational environment is constituted in a rich and interesting space to study, whether within enterprises or in established relations between companies (Vale et al, 2006, p. 47) without losing sight, in my understanding, of the relationships that go beyond the companies, encompassing ties with other organizations, such as those that make up the public sector and the third sector.

If before the private organizations were basically structured in a hierarchical way and with well-defined and delimited borders; if today they were focused on competitiveness and included in its internal environment, as already emphasized in this book, now they would have acquired more and more flexible structures, dilution of boundaries between their organizational and public spaces, and guidance with a focus on cooperation.

This causes the need to establish collective strategies, aimed to promote, according to Vale et al (2006, p. 46), relations of mutual trust, sense of purpose and collective work capacity, elements which underlie the concept of social capital.

The theoretical framework of social capital according to Vale et al (2006, p. 56), seems to be suitable for treatment of the organizational subject in several situations. The authors highlight the importance of this concept when understanding the current organizational environment - whose traditional concepts and practices are being questioned and revised, in favor of more interactive approaches . Then its use becomes not only adequate, but also fundamental.

Thus, Vale et al point out the organizational dynamics in the context marked by globalization, new technologies of information and communication, causing the revision of traditional organizational models. This scenario promotes greater concern for the quality of the internal environment, which needs to have more lean, decentralized and participatory structures, and greater interaction and collaboration with other organizations. (2006, p. 57)

The context I discuss in this book, Vale et al (2006, p. 59) bring another contribution to indicate ways of evaluating social capital in organizational networks and, therefore, take up the notion of measurement, to what they call vertical axis based on the intensity of union ties (bonding) that link, more intensely the company with certain segments, organizations and social groups generally located closer in physical, social or cultural sense.

The measurement indicated by the authors (Vale et al, 2006, p. 59) also includes the horizontal axis, which captures the bridges (bridging) that the company is able to establish with groups, organizations and diversified and more distant networks, that could be physical, social and cultural. According to the authors, this would also indicate:

(...) An increase of the social capital in the same was as companies intensify their contacts and interactions within their own home communities - enabling the proliferation of innovation based on tacit knowledge, present nature, between the companies present there, creating a greater local solidarity climate and the ability to implement collective action. But it occurs also an increase in the social capital , as the company broadened the scope, breadth and variety of its relations, making it possible to access remote resources, diverse and valuable ventures may exist on other networks and scenarios, and generating a flow of information between them. (Vale et al, 2006, p. 59)

These considerations are more than valid within a theme that aims to highlight the interface between organizational and public communication, once the social capital is at the essence of relationships that create ties between members, and make them commit to organizational and public interest issues.

However, it should be noted that even when presented with the indications of forms of measurement by Vale et al, it is not this book proposal to apply methods to assess social capital, although it considers important to its use in subsequent approaches.

To complete my analysis, it is necessary not only to highlight the importance of social capital in the organizational context, but also to take into account the democratic context, participation and civic engagement. Thus, Matos (2009, p. 44) precisely tries to emphasize and deepen the concept of social capital in the structuring of social ties and civic engagement. To this end, the author highlights Sennet´s work - which analyzes the corrosion of character and the decline of social capital.

As Sennet (cited Matos, 2009, p. 45) the character -above anything- designates the permanent features of our emotional experience, which is expressed by confidence and mutual engagement in an attempt to achieve the long-term goals, or even to delay gratification, with a view to a future goal.

Matos (2009, p. 45) notes that the work Sennet presents would help to clarify that the likely causes of corrosion are the same affecting social capital, bringing among other things, the reason why they should articulate personal and public interests.

A political system that does not provide humans the profound reasons for which interest for each other can not retain its legitimacy long (cited Matos, 2009, p. 45)

According to Putnam (cited Matos, 2009, p. 47) individuals are more likely to change their lives when they are part of a heavily engaged civic community. Thus, social ties and civic engagement have major influence on private and public life.

> "The interaction networks greatly widen the awareness of members, allowing them to develop an" I "and a " us", or, taking up the theoretical terms of rational choice, it can be said that the presence of these networks enhance the taste of individuals by collective benefits (Bevort and Lallement, cited Matos, 2009, p. 47)

So far I have tried to consider the concept of social capital, and its fields of application, as I have also demonstrated its usefulness to the organizational and democratic context; however, the role of communication in the formation of social capital still remains to be studied.

Matos (2009, p. 82), to address current perspectives of the conversation approach, remembers that the notions of public opinion and public sphere made the concept of conversation recognized as an important dimension of the establishment of democracy.

Matos (2009, p. 82) makes questions on why the talks are so important for the formation of democratic public spaces if, they are generally established in private contexts (little conducive for ideas debate) and among people who think similarly.

The author rescues different authors (Mansbridge, 1999; Kim and Kim, 2008; Moy and Gastil, 2006), and has pointed out that the talks tend to occur more often in environments where people feel protected to express their arguments. Then he concludes:

Take differing views on controversial contexts not only poses a challenge to individuals as well as a price: become a fluid conversation, friendly and pleasant in a clash of ideas aimed at producing an agreement or to solve a particular agreement or solving of an issue. (Matos, 2009, p. 82)

This approach particularly aligns to the concept of respect in the resolution, aspect treated in the previous chapter. However, Matos complements his analysis on the role of social capital conversation , and notes there is another form of conversation reported by Schudson as the one focused on problem solving, which approaches on the exchange of public arguments between people with different backgrounds, requiring participants to formulate their own views and respond to others' questions. (Matos, 2009, p. 84)

Evidence of communication for social capital is indicated by Matos (2009, p. 214) when quoting Hartman and Lenk (2001), he believes in its enhancing characteristic to achieve business goals, being an intangible asset capable to contribute social capital, as well as its nature.

Starting from the evidence that social capital and communication are interconnected, Matos suggests the concept of communicative capital, having as references Mulholland (2005) who proposes the combination of communication studies with social capital in order to understand how employees contribute to the growth of organizations (Matos, 2009, p. 214).

For Matos (2009, pp 216 -. 218), the application of the concept of social capital to organizational environment mainly to companies that aim to profit is necessary. Since organizational models are based on hierarchy, and strict rules of conduct and centralized authority have been increasingly questioned.

Therefore, private organizations need to be aligned with the democratic context, adjusting their models and strengthening their communication policies to contribute to social capital creation. For this, Matos suggests that insertion of communicative capital in a market environment brings a double possibility: on the one hand, we observe and analyze the concept between employees and the organization stakeholders in concrete action; in the other hand, we observe that under management rules, it demands efficient results from the communicative capital(2009, p. 218).

For Matos (2009, p. 218) the movement approach between the notion of social capital and the communication precisely offers the possibility to constitute individuals as citizens and civic actors, based on interactions that would allow social networks, either organizational and/or civic.

Finally, I believe that serving the public interest by different actors, including private organizations, requires the development of organizational and public communication policies, which depend on and influence the formation of social capital, facilitating citizen engagement in matters that affect the community by established trust bonds.

PART II

CHAPTER IV

1. Empirical research

In addition to the theoretical literature developed for this book, I also include empirical research that would allow an analysis of the interaction between organizational and public communication implemented in practice; it prospects this interaction increasingly adopted by companies .

Therefore, it is fundamental to remember that adopting a methodology is indispensable for the construction of science and for maximum approximation to the truth (Strelow, 2010, p.206), because its main goal is to emerge knowledge.

Despite knowing the importance that empirical research acquires in this work, one can not deny that there are difficulties and limitations for its development, as it happens with most research, after all, as alert Minayo (2000, p 197.):

"The researchers usually find three major obstacles when they leave for the analysis of data collected in the field (...) The first (...) 'illusion of transparency' (...) the second (...) succumb to the magic of the methods and techniques (...) the third (...) is the difficulty of joining theories and abstract concepts with the data collected in the field ".

To Cappelle et al (2003), research starts from the collected data (raw state), then it stops to establish procedures to systematize, categorize and make their analysis possible, to finally get to the searched results.

Cappelle et al (2003) also show that communications analysis have peculiarities, because the data can be collected through interviews, messages or documents in general.

Among the communications analysis mechanism one can find the content analysis I adopted: a theoretical and methodological mechanism applied to data obtained through interviews, messages and documents.

Content analysis takes the text as document restricted to be understood, and as an illustration of a delimited context situation, also based on its structure to be interpreted.

Still on content analysis, Cappelle et al claim that this methodology is widely used in communication analysis in the humanities and social sciences. (2003)

To Minayo (2000) content analysis is the most commonly adopted method in the treatment of qualitative research data. Already Silverman (1993) and Neumann (1994) consider it a set of quantitative techniques (cited Cappelle et al, 2003). While for Berg (1998), Insch et al (1997); Sarantakos (1993) content analysis has elements of both quantitative as qualitative approach (Quoted in Cappelle et al., 2003).

 I use quantitative and qualitative approach as a reference, which will provide the most comprehensive analysis since it includes textual emerging elements from the first stage of content analysis. This will also work on the data organization and systematization. Furthermore, it will include analytical phases to grasp the subjects social worldview, and related textual material from other authors.

Content analysis covers explanation initiatives, organization and expression of the message content, with the purpose of carrying out logical and explained deductions about the origin of these messages. It would also indicate who issued them, in what and/or which context is intended to cause effects through them. (Bardin, 1979)

The choice of this methodology is also given based on the assertion of Cappelle et al (2003), according to which the content analysis combines the rigor of being objective within the gift of subjectivity.

To Bardin (1979) and Minayo (2000) quantitative analysis turns to how often certain communication elements appear, concerned more with the development of new procedure forms to measure the identified meanings.

The qualitative approaches already turn to the presence or absence of a characteristic or set of characteristics in the analyzed messages, seeking to go beyond the merely descriptive range of quantitative techniques to achieve deeper interpretations based on inference. (Quoted in Cappelle et al, 2003)

Appolinário considers the content analysis as a set of scientific research techniques used in human sciences characterized by data analysis in which the fundamental elements of communication are identified, numbered and categorized (2009, p. 27).

Bardin (2009) states that any analysis must consider the organization, coding, categorization, inferences and the possibility of computer processing in its structure . This treatment can occur in three phases: statistical analysis (data classification, reorganization, transformation and description); aid in the studies and discoveries (variety, classes and distribution of data from a large amount of documents); and computer content analysis (making inferences on the social context of the collected data).

There are requirements for content analysis to be validated, as indicated by Freitas et al. (1997, p. 108). They are: quality of conceptual elaboration made a priori by the researcher; accuracy with which it will be translated into variables; analysis or categories scheme; and agreement between reality to be analyzed and these categories.

Considering the research that I look on at this book, I performed data collection with winning cases of the Exame Sustainability Guide[1] and

---

1   Exame Sustainability Guide is an annual publication of Editora Abril, which presents the ranking of companies that invest in sustainability initiatives.

ABERJE Award[2] (editions 2010, 2011, 2012 and 2013) that present interface between communication and sustainability; I selected a highlighted company in the 2013 edition of Exame Sustainability Guide and ABERJE Award and I monitored the posts on the social network called Facebook regarding to the selected company for content analysis. (November 2013 to March 2014).

The highlight company was awarded as Sustainable Company of the Year by Guia Exame Sustainability and Corporate Communication of the Year by ABERJE.

With regard to the procedures to systematize, categorize and make the analysis possible, I prefered to hire a company to use the BuzzMonitor program, with a survey of Facebook posts related to the Outstanding Company of the awards of the Exame Sustainability Guide and ABERJE in 2013 (From November / 2013 to March / 2014); I defined categories of analysis; I classified the posts into categories; and finally I analyzed the posts according to manifestation types and keywords.

The categories created included: 1-Bank´s word, 2-Bank´s reaction to client´s requests, 3-Client and general public word toward bank´s information, 4- Criticism messages and suggestions given by initiative from clients and general. Then types of expression (positive, negative or neutral) were quantified regarding to each stated category.

Following the qualitative analysis, I sought to relate the keywords Communication, Resolution, Dialogue, Debate / Discussion, Respect, Participation, Engagement, Citizenship Sustainability with the manifestations.

It fits here some clarification, as empirical research started with the survey of companies/projects awarded in the editions 2010, 2011, 2012 and 2013 Exame Sustainability Guide and ABERJE Award to scale the universe proposed for analysis.

---

2   ABERJE is the Brazilian Association of Corporate Communication, which for 40 years carries out annual awards of the best Brazilian business communication practices by professionals and organizations.

Later and as indicated above, I make the selection of cases that include -in their publicly available summaries- keywords related to this research topic.

Initially, I programmed conduct interviews with professionals in charge of projects in companies. However, after further readings and analysis of research methodologies in communication I came to the conclusion that more than the official voice, it was necessary to identify the manifestation of the different voices of the public, and their direct or indirect impact given by the actions and various companies. This study would contemplate the plurality emphasized in the theoretical approach.

Thus, starting from the assumption that the new social media have enabled individuals to turn into citizen-subjects and protagonists, I considered crucial to analyze the perception of those whose conduct and projects are developed by the companies.

Therefore, the selection of that company awarded in 2013 (Exame Sustainability Guide and ABERJE) for content analysis, proves to be essential and consistent with the theoretical basis of this work. Once the democratic context emphasized here requires the possibility that different voices manifest, these new technologies have made them increasingly possible.

At the same time, it is also clear that social networks monitoring could only occur in current projects, because it is proper to recent issues, and represented a limitation to the research of those from 2010, 2011 and 2012.

Thus, in order to consider the time efficacy that monitoring requires I completed the survey with the 2013 edition of the cases, and I chose to carry out the analysis on collected data from the company/project social network, which was highlighted in the latest edition competitions for the period of completion of this book.

Made these clarifications, I will now present the main data.

2. Main results - empirical research

Empirical research attempted to see the procedures on their social/ environmental and communication policies companies implement, and what changes have been incorporated to reveal their perception on social groups with whom they interact. To this end, three phases were developed:

2.1. First phase

For phase 1, the selection was made through a survey of companies that have their cases of social/environmental responsibility awarded and published by Guia Exame, in addition to the companies awarded by ABERJE by the 2010, 2011, 2012 and 2013 editions. Such pieces of information are available in print and online publication of Exame Sustainability Guide and in the ABERJE site.

The survey of cases Awarded by Guia Exame Sustainability and ABERJE Awards by the 2010, 2011, 2012 and 2013 editions, can be found in Appendix A, indicating the year of the award, winning companies and their projects.

The survey added up 178 cases, and from which were selected those that most clearly showed keywords related to communication, dialogue, engagement, deliberation, participation, debate / discussion, respect, citizenship and sustainability. My interest was to identify whether in the sustainability policies, communication is understood as an intertwining method between organizational actions and the public interest.

In this selection, it is possible to conclude that mentioned keywords occurred narrowly in the cases of the two events (Exame Sustainability Guide and ABERJE Award).

I also opted for making analytical treatment only to those companies that are mentioned in the award cases more than one keyword. This implies that with the keywords joint, we will then have more guarantees to the sense of such words.

2.2. Second phase[3]

Therefore in phase 2, the awarded projects in both competitions were selected; their corresponding keywords linked to this study were highlighted.

2.2.1. Analysis of projects[4]

Out of the 20 companies awarded in 2010, three leave the dialogue with the community significance explicit; however, there are those that promote their employees engagement , to turn them into multipliers, such as HSBC and Itaú Unibanco.

Alcoa, considered a sustainable company 2010, indicates as one of its actions the creation of a council to bring community , government and business altogether. In addition to the council meetings, which includes representatives of women, fishermen, government and the city officials and others, indirectly participate in the initiative through the technical chambers, which subsidizes the board with information about the environment, education, health and safety, among others. (Exame Sustainability Guide, 2010, p. 126)

As stated in the publication of the Exame Sustainability Guide (2010, p.127) "one of the most intense dialogue that the company has caught is with the Association of Communities of the Juruti Velho Region (Acorjuve). This reinforces the importance dedicated to communication, dialogue and participation, essential for sustainability policies and actions."

The Anglo-American - one of the companies awarded in 2010, also ensures in the publication that all social investments are defined along with the benefited population by the actions. Community participation in the suggested discussions has been growing. "Participation in the Community Forum Exchange has grown significantly," says the publication. (Exame Sustainability Guide, 2010, p. 134)

---

3   For analytical purposes, the 2013 edition was considered in the third stage, looking to highlight the company of the edition, both the Exame Sustainability Guide as the ABER-JE.
4   The quotes made in this session were taken out from Guide Exams Sustainability, editions 2010, 2011 and 2012.

Fibria - manufacturer of pulp and paper, which raised from the merger between Aracruz and VCP, among the awarded in 2010, invests in projects to generate income for the communities´ relationship of the 252 municipalities, where it has factories and plantations. However, what draws the most attention and allows to include it in this analysis is the fact that the company holds meetings with community residents to identify their main demands. (Exame Sustainability Guide, 2010, p. 146)

From the 21 companies considered 2011 sustainability models, the restricted ones are those that reinforce their commitment explicitly with the dialogue in joint with the community. One that stands out is Alcoa, which follows the same policy already highlighted in the 2010 edition.

According to the 2011 edition, every Alcoa assessment on the Juruti mine community impacts was done with the community participation (Exame Sustainability Guide 2011, p. 138). For Franklin Feder - Alcoa President - "we need to be always open to listen and dialogue without barriers". (Exame Sustainability Guide 2011, p. 138).

In the 2011 edition, Embraco, specializes in manufacturing compressors, states that they promote "sustainable development initiatives in the surrounding community, taking into account local peculiarities" (Exame Sustainability Guide 2011, p. 154). Noteworthy is the indication that the social investment performed is preceded by consultations with the affected communities to identify needs and strengthen community organization.

This same behavior seems to guide the actions of the "Laboratório Sabin" in Brasilia, also in the 2011 list, while ensuring that their "social investments are preceded by consultations with the communities affected by the initiative. It takes into account the potential for financial self-sufficiency projects and the generated learning by the initiative for the development and the improvement of public policies ". (Exame Sustainability Guide 2011, p. 176)

In the same way Anglo American, highlighted in the 2010 and 2011 editions, conquered in 2012 the title of Sustainable Company of the Year because, according to the publication (Exame Sustainability Guide 2012, p. 115) "established a dialogue with the community in the regions which it operates and reduced the environmental impact which it has been strategic for their expansion in the country. "

Emphasis can be given to the role of communication in the Anglo American sustainability project, with the already mentioned completion of the Community Forum Exchange, promoted by nickel mining unit to discuss publicly and openly the region company's action.

The AES dealership, winner of the event in other editions, appears in the 2012 award winning in guiding consumers in low-income neighborhoods on security measures, through an educational campaign.

Boticario (Brazilian Perfumes and creams store) appears in the list of the 2012 awarded companies, by stimulating its suppliers, franchisees and consumers to engage in sustainability initiatives.

From the 21 companies awarded in 2012, only three explicitly mention their concern with communication focused on dialogue with their stakeholders, to define their social or environmental policies.

Clearly, for some of the companies that do not include communication in the relationship, this can be placed strategically in their social practices. However, as there was no direct mention, I chose not to mention them in this analysis, since my proposal is to identify if the communication focused on participation and exercise of citizenship integrates organizational objectives.

It is also noticeable in many cases that organizational communication is still understood as a practice linked more to the diffusion than to dialogue, being established unilaterally, without regard to the dialogue, participation and encouragement to the resolution of social policies and social groups integrated of citizens and subjects of the process.

From the awards held by ABERJE, I highlighted some of the cases that connect communication with social, community and relationship projects. Considering the presence of keywords, we have as a result the following analysis:

The project Sustainable Awareness Fiat in 2011, focused on the internal audience, establishing debate on sustainability. The project was based on five pillars, on which the Fiat builds its understanding of sustainability at the same time as it attempted to disclose them and seek employee engagement (products, people, community, partners, planet).

This case, where the company is stimulating debate and engagement of the internal public, illustrates one of the possibilities to make organizational environment more aligned and consistent with the context of a society that is based on deliberative democratic policies.

In another case, the Petrobras Project called Ilhas do Rio awarded in 2012, highlights the partnerships with civil society groups and public and private sectors, ensuring the planned activities sustainability . Partnerships, in my view, presuppose dialogue and participation, which highlight the perspective of a communication policy in the defense bases in which I do this work.

In the category - Communication and relationship with society - I highlighted in 2012 the project House Imerys - Pigments for Paper, in Barcarena, Pará.

For the construction of the House Imerys, to establish dialogue was necessary. The new project communication was made during five months in meetings with community leaders and local institutions that were somehow linked to social projects.

This was also presented to employees of the company. Professionals in the company gradually began to present themselves as volunteers to the project - after all, many live in Barena, including Vila do Conde, and they saw a way to benefit the community where they live. Using his skills in carpentry, electrical and plumbing, they moved during working hours to help build the House Imerys.

This example features quite explicitly that the bond can be established between the private sphere and the public sphere, and at the same time strengthens the social role of the company to encourage the development of their staff, particularly as citizens.

The 2011 edition of ABERJE awards highlights the project AngloGold Ashanti - Dialogue expanded with stakeholders, which it used the process of communication and dialogue as a way to improve the relationship with stakeholders.

In 2010, the company deepened and strengthened the process of stakeholders engagement through Expanded Dialogue Meetings.

The project focus was to establish a structured and systematic mechanism to hear and understand the needs of stakeholders, transforming these contributions on improvement opportunities in their area, and at the same time, promoting the engagement of these stakeholders, seeking alignment and plumbing for common goals.

Therefore, according to the case description, a meeting was held to listen to the people and establish a frank and open dialogue; they shared experiences and perceptions, aligned and deepened the concepts and practices of sustainability of AngloGold Ashanti Brazil; the reflection on the Political Organization of Social Responsibility and the role of each participant of this journey was stimulated; it identified opportunities for improvement.

Vale was also awarded in 2011 by ABERJE in the category Communications and Community Relations for his project Communicators Network, which included the creation of qualified spaces for dialogue. It also encouraged the participation of communities in many different opportunities to conduct open and transparent dialogues, capable to make the company proposals public .

Therefore, Social Licensing - an innovative approach was used. It allowed the company and the environmental agency promote a participatory and transparent licensing process.

In this context, in line with the values of Vale, an extensive process of social dialogue began, which aimed to promote interaction spaces from conducting activities guided by open exchange of participatory information between the environmental agency (licensor), business (licensed) and communities (civil society). While the discussions have contributed to increase the social capital of the region.

What characterizes these award-winning cases is the emphasis on dialogue, debate, participation, engagement, demonstrating that is beginning to be a concern for the alignment of organizational policies to public policies. With this perspective within the democratic context, communication policies are required to contribute to the establishment of links between the public interest and the private interest, even because it is through communication that relationships are established and encourage social links.

2.3.Third phase

Even with the undeniable contribution of the analysis above, I thought important to complement my remarks, as I have argued before with an analysis that is also considered the manifestation perspective not only from the company but also from its stakeholders. Hence the selection, among the companies listed in the initial survey, the company of the year according to Guia Exame Sustainability and ABERJE Award.

This selection also included "the present" criteria, since the proposal was to identify the manifestations of customers and the general public on the social network - Facebook, which required a choice based on a recent project.

Thus, the survey period for the post selection was conducted from November / 2013, when the award of Itaú / Unibanco as Sustainable Company of the

Year by Guia Exame Sustainability and Communications Company of the year by ABERJE was announced.

The month setting March / 2014 as limit to the survey was due to this work completion deadline scheduled for the month of April, which determined the time between data collection and analysis.

Considering the posts distributed between the categories already defined: 1-Bank´s word, 2-Bank´s reaction to client´s requests, 3-Client and general public word toward bank´s information, 4- Criticism messages and suggestions given by initiative from clients and general. Within these categories, the types of manifestation were calculated as positive, negative, and neutral.

Thus, as can be seen in the graphs, when the Bank is manifested either in category 1 or category 2, its posture is considered positive and expressed in words as: Communication, Consultation, Culture, Debate, Deliberation, Dialogue, Engagement, Interaction, Ombudsman, Participation, Environmental Protection, Social Responsibility, Sustainability (and their derivations).

Here's an example of posting that fits in Category 1:

Figure 1. Example of posting category 1

In category 1, 81 publications between the months of November / 2013 to March / 2014 were analyzed , a percentage equal to 100% of total publications.

The following graph shows the category 1 and the type of manifestation per month, in the mentioned period:

Graph 1 - Bank word (Information released by the bank): all months 100% positive.

Active filters: Customized period. (01/11/2013 to 31/03/2014), Facebook, Positive, Neutral, Negative, Mixed, 81 posts)

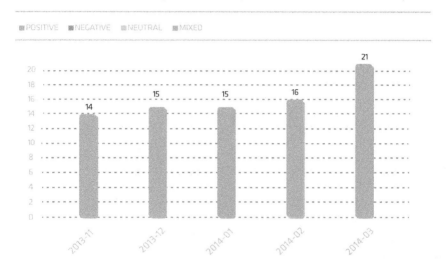

In category 2, 4925 publications were analyzed between the months of November / 2013 to March / 2014, a percentage equivalent to 100% of total period publications.

Following the graph for category 2 and the type of manifestation, divided by month:

Graph 2 - Bank word (Answers given to requests made by customers and public in general)

Active filters: Customized period. (01/11/2013 to 31/03/2014), Facebook, Positive, Neutral, Negative, Mixed, 4,925 posts)

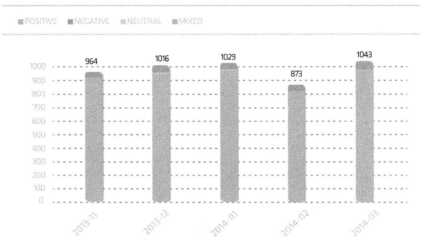

For category 2 in November / 2013, there was 96% of positive manifestations and 04% considered as negative. In December, there were 94% of manifestations considered positive, against 06% negative. In January 2014, the positive manifestations were 96%, while 04% were negative. In February and March 2014 the percentages were the same: 94% positive, against 06% negative.

These data shows that in both, both categories which represent the Bank word, show that the types of manifestations are considered highly positive, probably reflecting the communication policy, either at the time the Bank releases information for customers and the general public, as in times when responding to requests from customers and the general public, indicating conduct that serves a formal dialogue guidance, based on respect; in other words, the way the company communicates impacts influencing opinion and building up its image, reputation and brand.

In category 1, the positive manifestation rate is 100%. Even in category 2, regarding to Bank's posts, in order to respond to customers and citizens, the positive rate is very significant, and what appears as "negative" does not convey as a bad approach from the bank - but simply that it did not know how to meet the expectations of the people who claim.

Here's an example of a post referred to the category 2:

□ 🄵® **Itaú** Alex, we respect your opinion and we are always open...

Alex, we respect your opinion and are we we are always open to comments and suggestions like yours. We believe that education, culture, sport and urban mobility are important pillars to change society for the better. And we would like to take this message to talk about some of our initiatives in this direction;-). One of our favorite projects is the "Read to a child" campaign, which distributes free children's booklets for customers and non-customers. It is an incentive for children develop their imagination and their ability to learn reading, which in the long term contributes to they become more creative, educated and aware adults. On the issue of urban mobility, our main delivery is the bike sharing project that provides borrowed bikes in cities across the country. The idea is that they are used for short trips on a daily basis and thus contribute to the improvement of the metropolises. Also we believe in bringing more culture and sports to the people (always good, right?), And that's why we support events like the Curitiba Theater Festival, the Fair Literary Festival, Rio Open, the World Cup and others, and, of course, the installations of Itaú Culture and Itaú Films space throughout Brazil :-) Also, we have important projects going on in the Itaú Social Foundation and Unibanco Institute which work to contribute to improving the quality of Brazilian public education. Any questions, is just writing to us. We will have great pleasure in continuing this conversation :-) Sincerely!

2014-03-31 11:49:00 👍 0 likes

Figure 2 - Example of posting - Category 2

In category 3, 28,951 publications between the months of November 2013 to March 2014 were analyzed , a percentage equal to 100% of total publications.

The following graph shows the category 3 and the type of manifestation, divided by month, from November 2013 to March 2014:

Graph 3 - Customer and Public in General Word (Responses as the Bank issues information)

Active filters: Customized period. (01/11/2013 to 31/03/2014), Facebook, Positive, Neutral, Negative, Mixed, 28,951 posts)

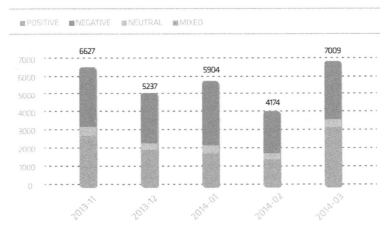

In category 3, in November 2013, there were 44% of manifestation considered positive, 07% neutral and 49% negative. In December 2013 there were 38% positive manifestations, 07% neutral and 55% negative. In January 2014, the manifestation were 30% positive, 07% neutral, while 63% were considered negative. In February 2014 there were 33% positive, 09% neutral and 58% negative. In March 2014, the percentages were 48% positive, 06% neutral and 45% negative.

Some examples of posts applied to this category:

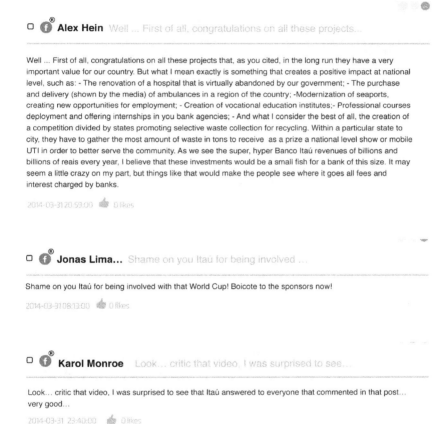

☐ **Alex Hein** Well ... First of all, congratulations on all these projects...

Well ... First of all, congratulations on all these projects that, as you cited, in the long run they have a very important value for our country. But what I mean exactly is something that creates a positive impact at national level, such as: - The renovation of a hospital that is virtually abandoned by our government; - The purchase and delivery (shown by the media) of ambulances in a region of the country; -Modernization of seaports, creating new opportunities for employment; - Creation of vocational education institutes;- Professional courses deployment and offering internships in you bank agencies; - And what I consider the best of all, the creation of a competition divided by states promoting selective waste collection for recycling. Within a particular state to city, they have to gather the most amount of waste in tons to receive as a prize a national level show or mobile UTI in order to better serve the community. As we see the super, hyper Banco Itaú revenues of billions and billions of reais every year, I believe that these investments would be a small fish for a bank of this size. It may seem a little crazy on my part, but things like that would make the people see where it goes all fees and interest charged by banks.

2014-03-31 20:59:00 0 likes

☐ **Jonas Lima...** Shame on you Itaú for being involved ...

Shame on you Itaú for being involved with that World Cup! Boicote to the sponsors now!

2014-03-31 08:13:00 0 likes

☐ **Karol Monroe** Look... critic that video, I was surprised to see...

Look... critic that video, I was surprised to see that Itaú answered to everyone that commented in that post... very good...

2014-03-31 23:40:00 0 likes

Figure 3 - Posts examples - category 3

Finally, in category 4 19,846 publications between the months of November/2013 to March/2014 were analyzed, percentage also equivalent to 100% of total publications.

The chart below shows the category 4, the type of manifestation and its division by month, from November/2013 to March/2014:

Graph 4 - Criticism messages and suggestions given by initiative from clients and general.

Active filters: Customized period. (01/11/2013 to 31/03/2014). Facebook, Positive, Neutral, Negative, Mixed, 19,846 posts)

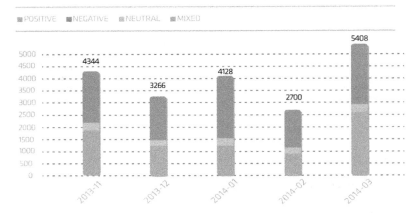

In category 4, there were 42% positive demonstrations in November, 07% neutral and 50% negative. In December there were 39% positive manifestations, 07% neutral and 54% negative. In January, the demonstrations amounted to 31% positive, 08% neutral and 61% negative. In February there were 36% positive, 08% neutral and 56% negative. In March the percentages were 46% positive, 06% neutral and 48% negative.

The following are examples of posts for each type of manifestation of this category:

☐ **Andrew Goodman..** I WAS HAMPERED BY ITAÚ BANK ...

I WAS HAMPERED BY ITAÚ BANK ... the LOSS and THEFT INSURANCE is optional and not mandatory, which is being offered by the management of credit cards and guaranteed by an insurance company. The insurance must cover the withdrawals and purchases from the misuse of a non-authorized THIRD party. The credit card contract and agreements contain clauses indicating that the managers blame the holder / associated by the misuse a prior communication with bank call center. However, the Consumer Protection Code considers such improper procedure, since the responsibility for safety of service is also from the provider, which should take care when accepting credit or debit card payments for products or services. It is worth mentioning even though under the law the consumer is vulnerable and the fragile system allows sometimes no authorized use of credit or debit cards by third parties. The consumer should formalize its claims in a consumer protection organ such as Special Civil Court (values up to 20 minimum wages) or ordinary courts.

2014-03-31 21:48:00   0 likes

Type of negative manifestation - Category 3

☐ **Lucy Mariane...** Beautiful, it would be to see these ...

Beautiful, it would be to see these "Brazilian fans" united for EDUCATION, HEALTHCARE AND SECURITY, saying NO to corruption, impunity, scams, depredation, violence, bad politicians and injustices that happen in our country!

2014-14-31 10:47:00   0 likes

Type of neutral expression - Category 3

68

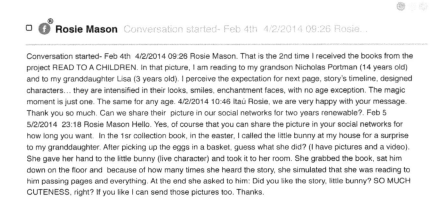

Conversation started- Feb 4th 4/2/2014 09:26 Rosie Mason. That is the 2nd time I received the books from the project READ TO A CHILDREN. In that picture, I am reading to my grandson Nicholas Portman (14 years old) and to my granddaughter Lisa (3 years old). I perceive the expectation for next page, story's timeline, designed characters... they are intensified in their looks, smiles, enchantment faces, with no age exception. The magic moment is just one. The same for any age. 4/2/2014 10:46 Itaú Rosie, we are very happy with your message. Thank you so much. Can we share their picture in our social networks for two years renewable?. Feb 5 5/2/2014 23:18 Rosie Mason Hello. Yes, of course that you can share the picture in your social networks for how long you want. In the 1sr collection book, in the easter, I called the little bunny at my house for a surprise to my granddaughter. After picking up the eggs in a basket, guess what she did? (I have pictures and a video). She gave her hand to the little bunny (live character) and took it to her room. She grabbed the book, sat him down on the floor and because of how many times she heard the story, she simulated that she was reading to him passing pages and everything. At the end she asked to him: Did you like the story, little bunny? SO MUCH CUTENESS, right? If you like I can send those pictures too. Thanks.

2014-03-31 12:28:00   👍 0 likes   💬 1 comment

Figure 4 - Examples of posts - Category 4

Type of positive manifestation - Category 3

There is thus a balance between the types of manifestation during the months of the survey, both Category 3 (Customer and Public in General Word - replies in relation to the Bank's information releases), and for category 4 (Criticism messages and suggestions given by initiative from clients and general).

At the same time, we realize that when it comes to customers and the general public, the negative words that stand out are indignation, dissatisfaction, anger, abuse, theft, deceit, bad, and loss.

There is also the use of slang terms with some frequency, indicating that many who are manifested in social networks about the Bank do it disrespectfully; this might perhaps have been driven by problems related to lack of proper expected customer attention, or even by the freedom of speech that social networks seem to suggest.

Another aspect to be emphasized with regard to the number of posts that appear classified in categories 3 and 4, It is that is significantly higher than those that comprise categories 1 and 2. This indicates that when it comes about present critics and problems, there is a much greater manifestation trend. Therefore, there is need of attention so that communication policies are geared to monitoring, listening and understanding the negative manifestations, and investing in initiatives that promote dialogue and approach.

It can be seen that there are six types of posts:

1- Those who complain about the poor quality of what the Itaú Bank offers to its customers;

2- Those who praise the Bank, noting that it well attended the individual complaints, mainly just the case of the claimant in particular;

3- Those who were moved by the Advertising Campaign that the Bank sponsored regarding to the Football World Cup;

4- Those who complain about the money spent on the costs of this World Cup - seen as a money coming out of people's pocket with non apparent social benefits;

5- Those that are just pure mockery;

6-Those that connect the banks to the group of corrupt politicians who harm the country, establishing a bond between them.

Here are some random examples:

□ **Erick Mott** the most disgusting bank in the ...

the most disgusting bank in the world. Too much bureaucracy to open an account, even digital, signatures and many other things. At the moment I asked for a loan they did not authorized it, but when a stranger does so using my name, with no signatures, not even the digital one, he gets R$ 2,500. Fuck you. Worst thing I did so far. Now I am going to suit them.

2014-03-29 16:31:00   0 likes

Figure 5 - Type of negative manifestation - Category 4

□ **John García** Whoever who watches that advertisement ...

Whoever who watches that advertisement must think that the Brazilian citizen has conditions to go and participate in that shitty world cup.Just check out the ticket prices. Without considering that it will be done with the sweat of the people that will never go to a decent school, quality hospitals and use acceptable public transportation. It just make me furious.

2014-03-28 07:46:00   0 likes

Figure 6 - Type of negative manifestation - Category 3

□ **Philips S Woodman** World cup for the filthy rich, the lower...

World cup for the filthy rich, the lower class goes to fuck itself working, gets together to fight for its equal rights and no for that corruption trashcan. _I_ Suck my dick!!!!

2014-03 26 21:08:00   0 likes

Figure 7 - Type of negative manifestation - Category 3

Adriane Serrato People, I am not against this...

People, I am not against this, but I would like to tell my experience with Itaú. I have 3 accounts, I am a customer since 1990 and all I ask is to be nicely attended, my bank managers are very competent and listeners, therefore Itaú works for me.

2014-03-29 08:12:00 0 likes

Figure 8 - Type of positive manifestation - Category 3

Brooke Rodrigo Sullivar I saw a lot of claims, but so far I just can tell...

I saw a lot of claims, but so far I just can tell about this bank good things. I always had been well treated, but it would be better if the fees were not so high. I hope it continues being this good so I don't have to change banks again.

2014-03-28 13:01:00 0 likes

Figure 9 - Type of positive manifestation - Category 3

Edison Marino I am Itaú customer for 15 years...

I am Itaú customer for 15 years and I have been always well treated by the managers that always inform about the best application. I am a small investors and I have never had a problem...Let's enjoy the music and if you have problems with bank, call them and solve it.

2014-03-26 07:47:00 0 likes

Figure 10 - Type of positive manifestation - Category 3

☐ **Fabiola Gross..** After several attempts solving ...

After several attempts solving a problem being very friendly (I called the SAC, counting the total of 10 protocols, more than 2 calls on the phone of 30 hours that was informed in here (that was not provided in the protocol) and two more protocols with the customer attention call-center. All this besides all the claims I also made in the official Itaú Bank webpage here in Facebook and in their website "claims here" where in neither of them the PROBLEM WAS NOT RESOLVED.The bank in retaliation for all this claims, it closed my account WITH ANY PREVIOUS INFORMATION and my money just disappear from my account. After uncountable calls to know where my money was, I received a call yesterday (13/1/14) from their call-center telling me that my account was closed due "commercial disagreement" and that the money was in a Registered Letter (saying that my account was closed) with a Payment Order from the Itaú Bank. This is a total ABSURD! Since there was not an friendly understanding from Itaú Bank I will have to take other measures. Just one word for all this: SHAME ON YOU!

2014-01-14 17:43:00 👍 0 likes

Figure 11 - Type of negative manifestation - Category 4

☐ **July Kan** The name of your love 1- Close your hand 2- ...

The name of your love 1- Close your hand 2- Say the name of one day of the week 3- Your name 4- Open your hand 5- Copy and paste this in other 15 comments, and right in the day you chose, that person will tell you that he or she likes you and will ask you to be boyfriend or girlfriend.If you reject to post this, everything will go wrong for the next 3 years.

2014-02-02 21:24:00 👍 0 likes

Figure 12 - Type of random post

The post above exemplifies approaches on random issues between manifestations on issues related to the Bank.

☐ **Kate Rodriguez**  15 year old girl received a facebook ...

15 year old girl received a facebook message. She deleted it and she didn't even read it. All this because it talked about Jesus telling her: Daughter, I sent you this message because tomorrow can be too late. The little girl laugh with irony and said: "what a lie!". In the next day she did not wake up because she died, but before she left a note saying: Do not ignore Jesus, may be he was not the one who wrote to me but it was him who sent this to test you. If you love God, send this message to 20 people. Now you are one count! In 9 minutes, something is going to make you happy. Everything in life are just details....I hope you really read it, since it is from my heart! I just passing by to tell you that something really good happened to me. Today I received the message below, and when I was starting to send it to other people, I received a great news! I hope it works with you too! PSalm 100:4 says: God has seen your fights. God says that they are coming to an end. A blessing is coming to your direction, if you believe in it....

2014-03-31 21:10:00 👍 0 likes

Figure 13 - Type of random post

The following is another post that exemplifies several approaches of random questions between manifestations on issues related to the Bank.

☐ **Sarah Fernandez** He: Do you think I am handsome? She: No. He: Am I ...

He: Do you think I am handsome? She: No. He: Am I in your heart? She: No. He: Will you cry for me? She: No. He: (the sad lover turned around to leave). She grabbed his arm and said: I don't want u, I desire u, I don't think u are handsome, u are beautiful, u are not in my heart, u are my heart, I would not cry for u, I would die for u. Today at midnight the person u love will perceive your feelings Something nice will happen between 1 and 4 pm wherever you are: at the internet, at school, at work... If you break this chain you will have bad luck for 10 relationships for 10 years....Once you copy and paste in 20 comments and , right away, you press F9 it will appear the initial letter of the boy or girl that loves you.

2014-02-09 20:33:00 👍 0 likes

Figure 14 - Another post that exemplifies several approaches of random questions between events on issues related to the Bank.

Although it may be considered a survey of an ephemeral reality, there is no doubt that Internet, especially social media, has revealed itself as a phenomenon that impacts public and private institutions by increasing manifestations of several scattered voices, many of them experiencing only recently the opportunity to deliver their opinions, whether positive or negative about topics from various natures.

Among these topics, some may be characterized as intimate while others relate to matters of public interest. What matters is that people express themselves without the need of intermediaries which empowers the citizens, in a way that they feel more urged to give their opinion on various issues, especially when those affect their life.

This phenomenon therefore can not be seen strictly as an object in this research, but above all, as the responsible for generating impact on the amount and diversity of given opinions .

In other ways, we would hardly have the opportunity to raise the large number of manifestations of expression that arise in social media, as shown in this book.

Consequently It is undeniable that the presence of social networks provokes the rise of new paradigms for communication, and relationship between organizations and social groups.

This same phenomenon reveals its democratic face, and exemplifies how the boundaries between public and private are becoming hybrid. As formal and respectful way or as informal, banal and / or aggressively, people have spoken out about conducting companies and demanding responsibility for their decisions, contrary to what before was restricted to their private sphere.

Such company decisions currently create judgments, whether positive, negative or neutral, from a growing number of people who are no longer recipients and objects of communication policies. Now they are transformed into subjects, actors and protagonists with the right to speak.

The survey shown that the companies seem to have understood this new scenario, which incorporates the new interlocutor subject. However, there are still many organizations that get surprised though they are not prepared to adopt policies and communication practices aligned with the democratic context.

In the case of Itaú / Unibanco, you see the use of communication channels that encourage dialogue, with guidance so that all triggered as information on their initiatives and policies takes place in an open and respectful manner.

It is obvious that the Bank, as a financial institution, has to worry about its reputation and how it builds and consolidates its brand in a competitive market and society that demands justification for their profits.

It must be also mentioned that the choice for analyzing Itaú / Unibanco was due to their awards in two exhibitions: 2013 (Sustainable Company of the Year by Exame Sustainability Guide and Corporate Communication of the Year by ABERJE).

However, it was rare the posts on that topic during the survey that directly dealt with the award-winning projects in any of the categories of analysis, even though the monitoring has been started from the month when the respective awards happened.

This indicates that even getting recognition from the awards´ judges and promoters, from groups linked more directly to this type of events and who had access to the cases publication, especially through print and electronic versions of Exame Sustainability Guide and website ABERJE, the awards did not generate great impact in the demonstrations (positive or negative) on social networks, indicating that there are social/environmental projects that do not necessarily have significant dialogue with their audiences.

It is shown, thus, a kind of inconsistency, since such projects would require dialogue with at least those who are impacted by their actions; also assuming the need spaces existence for deliberation in organizational environments to define the so called social/environmental projects.

As the proposal of empirical research was to observe the company's development and execution in their social/environmental and communication policies, and what changes have been incorporated, revealing their perception regarding to social groups with whom they interact. We can say, specifically in the case of Itaú/Unibanco, this entanglement did not exist.

Of course we must also take into account that some of Bank projects were aimed to the internal audience, and this made the manifestation in social networks more difficult. The inconsistency still remains, such is the case of application of the public communication concept due to the difficulty in the social networks manifestations.

However, one can not ignore that the demonstrations are not of exclusive responsibility of the Bank. Since the individual must be today the subject of the communication process, it is also up to him or her the responsibility for the issues of collective interest demonstrations.

From the posts presented, it is possible to identify a significant number attached to self-interest issues, in order to expose problems related to services offered by the Bank or even questions about charges and fees, which is also legitimate.

What can be seen from demonstrations related to public interest matters are those related to perceptions of developed cultural projects (Itaú Cultural), or even about sponsorship from the Bank, with particular emphasis on the World Cup 2014.

In this case, there are demonstrations of approval and disapproval because there was a tendency to regard the sponsors, including Itaú, as being responsible for holding the World Cup in Brazil. This involved both profits for the image, reputation and brand of the sponsoring company, by those who see the positive aspects of the event, as well as questions and criticism from those who considered it a harmful event to the country and its people.

However, the analysis of phase 2 of this research has identified companies that demonstrate concern about key issues, with the inclusion of arguments that reinforce the presence of dialogue, consultation, debate, engagement, and customer attention. And all of these issues are crucial to ensure that companies undertake social/environmental projects maintaining interfaces with communication.

3. Relationship between the research analyzes and the hypothesis

Among the hypotheses that guided this book, it was possible to partially prove by empirical research that the interrelationship of organizational communication with the public communication tends to align the interests of the market and the State. This hypothesis was particularly evidenced by the survey and analysis performed in phase 2, when some of the companies reported in their cases the adoption of practices to encourage participation, dialogue, engagement, debate, customer service, prior to definition of its social projects.

The outcome of empirical research was that there is no evidence that in a democratic society, when the organizational communication includes public communication as a fundamental concept of the public sphere, it would exists the tendency of recognition of stakeholders, professional communication and society. However, there has been acknowledgement of projects with the awards, involving judges, organizations directly linked to the event and those who had access to the company publications.

Still, the recognition does not happen necessarily due to the communication these awarded companies include Public Communication as a key concept.

The hypothesis that considered organizational communication policies can contribute with public communication, when they are reflected in the private sphere as well as in the public, could be proven through empirical research by observing both the second, and the third phase.

In the second phase, with the different companies´ analysis that included in their cases keywords related to debate, deliberation, dialogue, engagement, participation, customer service, it became apparent that organizations' concern are more aligned with the democratic scenario and with the impact generated on the public sphere.

In the third phase of the research, with the analysis of posts on Itaú / Unibanco, one can observe the Bank's concern to present their practices geared to social, environmental, cultural and quality of life, which shows a behavior turned to justify their action within society, thus reflecting a communication policy that generates impact in the public sphere.

As for the hypothesis those companies that adopt integrated organizational communication policies, non restrictive to market results, are those that generate positive impact in the public sphere. They have more strategic and comprehensive view of its commitment to the issues of public interest. So forth, it can be analyzed that under a theoretical point of view, the hypothesis can be proven. This does not happen under the empirical point of view, although there are signs that the social/environmental projects developed until now yet lack of an effective proof, such as the completion of new researches to assessing in depth communication policies adopted by such companies.

Under the last hypothesis, related to the actions that stimulate the manifestation, debate and interaction between organizations and social groups, they have been part of the communication policies in companies, social institutions and public institutions; they have also shown the links between organizational communication and public communication proven under a the theoretical point of view, and in a relative manner in the empirical researches. The manifestation space is present regardless of the stimulus provided by the companies, due to the advent of social media.

However, one can not deny that there are companies creating manifestation spaces, as exemplified in the second phase of this research. These spaces are in the form of forums, councils, meetings and gatherings.

PART III

1. Conclusions

If democracy presupposes citizen participation in the discussions that affect their lives, the concept of public communication is revealed in line with the deliberation. It is in this context that democratic discussions can influence the legislative process. Such discussions can be drawn from conversations that occur in both private and public spheres, producing collective results.

Of course, society needs the establishment of criteria to define what in the private sphere should be discussed and deliberated about the public sphere, so as not to compromise individual freedom. However, there is no doubt that many issues that present themselves in the public sphere arise from the problems that citizens face in their daily lives.

In a democratic society the boundary between public and private tends to blur, as private organizations also need to be aligned with the democratic scenario, being willing to create deliberation spaces that allow the manifestation of the arguments of those who related to it, with respect and equal consideration.

In this context, it is important to highlight the respect since it is crucial to ensure arguments in a more open way. Guiding the level and quality of the discussion, which will influence the processes of deliberation and determination, the result of an effective democratic debate would be considered and arose from various manifestation spaces.

The analysis presented here tried to align the interrelationship between the concepts of public and organizational communication with democracy, deliberation and social capital.

From the hypothesis considered for this book, it can be verified by a theoretical approach that organizational communication integrates to public communication as a fundamental concept, aligning the market and State interests, when this is developing environmental/sustainability responsibility policies. Therefore , it serves the interests of all, including medium and long-term company interests.

It was also theoretically possible to prove the hypothesis that, in a democratic society when the Organizational Communication includes Public Communication as a fundamental concept of the public sphere, there is the tendency of recognition from stakeholders, professionals in communication and society.

However, this hypothesis can not be proven by empirical research, as already analyzed in the survey conducted in the social network called Facebook, there have not existed manifestation that matched the dialogue between the company and the public specifically about the winning projects aforementioned.

This can cause serious question about the real objectives of such projects, since the lack of pronouncement about the awarded initiatives can express a concern of a lot more focused companies to generate value from investors than broader concern for all stakeholders, especially those who will be most directly impacted by these actions.

In this sense, the suggestion to these prizes'organizers is important. It aimed at awarding companies to focus on environmental responsibility and communication, to include criteria that also evaluate the spaces of dialogue and stimulus for expression, debate and deliberation, created by organizations in defining, planning and execution its social and environmental responsibility policies.

Similarly, affirmations that organizational communication policies can contribute to public communication and that such policies can generate positive impacts in the public sphere, also defined as hypothesis could be confirmed in theory; however, it empirically had limited demonstrations, precisely due to the absence of explicit deliberation spaces.

Finally, it became clear those actions that stimulate the manifestation, debate and interaction between organizations and social groups, part of the communication policies of some companies. This has been highlighted in Phase 2 and Phase 3 of the empirical research of this book. It also showed the intertwining between Organizational Communication and Public Communication still requiring maturity , begins to manifest in a embryonic form, particularly because of the dialogue with the advent of social media.

Thus, with both theoretical and empirical analyses, it can be concluded the organizational communication and public communication concepts increasingly tend to intertwine in a context that requires the organization interests align with those from society. Although, this concept proves limited recurrence in most of the companies analyzed here.

This trend also suggests that communication policies should take into account key issues such as ensuring the participation of all the organizational level, considering democracy must go beyond the State sphere.

These communication policies also need to consider their role in building the social capital, because the established social ties based on trust account not only economic gains for the company, but also represent the way they strengthen the different groups, the public spheres. Therefore, one has to recognize the new role of individuals and social groups in society.

Some companies, as can be seen in phase 2 of the empirical research, not only include concern for the public interest, as they have also set up communication policies that allow consultation and the manifestation of the community involved.

From all the foregoing and considering the analysis of levels of organizational consciousness proposed by Richard Barrett (1998), who I mentioned in section 4, it can be concluded that companies that appear in the first levels, especially those at level 1, (that focus on financial issues and organizational growth, including values such as profitability, shareholder value, employee health and safety) maintain distance between organizational communication and public communication, as their financial interests appear above the public interest.

At level 2, focusing on relationships (which includes the quality of interpersonal relationships between employees and customers/suppliers and values such as open communication, conflict resolution, customer satisfaction, courtesy and respect) there are prospects of evolving from an organizational communication restricted to the domestic level, to a communication involving a public interest bias. However, this has its limitations regarding to the appearance of fears related to loss of control and personal consideration because this generates manipulation, guilt and internal competition.

Level 3, Self-Esteem, also reveals potential that Organizational Communication evolves to a public perspective, although limiting, since there is concern about management practices that improve the working methods and the delivery of services and products, including values such as productivity, efficiency, professional growth, skills development and quality. But it also presents problems arising from present values as status, arrogance, bureaucracy and complacency.

Level 4 also shows potential for the establishment of organizational communication policies at a more advanced level of interaction. It aims to continuous renewal and the development of new products and services, and contains values that overlap the potentially limiting values in levels 1 and 3.

Values at this level include liability, employee participation, learning, innovation, teamwork, personal development and knowledge sharing. These are preconditions for the beginning of social capital development and future prospects of engagement in matters of public interest.

Level 5, in turn, focuses on community spirit in the company. It includes values such as trust, integrity, honesty, awareness of values, cooperation, excellence and justice. It highlights that this level is the most suitable to the creation of social capital, which can also be understood as a preparation level for the further advancement, across organizational boundaries.

The level 6, which turns to the maturing and strengthening of relationships and employees self-realization, also integrates the levels that favor the development of social capital. As this level involves the internal and external environment, because within the organization includes values such as leadership development, ability to mentor, ability coach and employees self realization; it externally includes values such as collaboration with customers and suppliers, building partnerships, strategic alliances, community involvement, environmental awareness and make a difference. It can be considered as the level that can show the relationship between internal and external, between private and public spheres.

However, it is level 7 that achieves, more effectively to reflect the highest level of internal and external connection, since within the organization includes values such as vision, wisdom, ability to forgive and compassion and externally include values such as social justice, human rights, global perspective and future generations.

With this analysis, it can be concluded that the interaction between public communication and organizational communication is not yet a practically understood by all organizations, because this relationship depends precisely from the level of consciousness of each organization.

It is worth emphasizing that in the current democratic context and of citizenship is inconceivable that the development of actions or social responsibility, environmental and communication policies do not promote openness to participation, debate and spaces for deliberation involving collective subjects affected by these decisions.

This context requires that communication must no longer be just a tool and be a management policy, where everyone directly or indirectly must exercise the right and the duty to express themselves, to participate, to position and to take responsibility in relation to the decisions that will help the public space.

Finally, it should be noted that, as regards the empirical analysis, the survey conducted in this publication had its limitations, especially in the phase involving the monitoring of the social network called Facebook, due its restriction when gathering data about a company. Still, we believe that this work brings effective contributions to the design of new studies to deepen the approach proposed here.

GLOSSARY

Accountability: A term that lacks conceptual homogeneity. It is often used in circumstances denoting civil responsibility, liability, obligations and balances presentation. In administration, *accountability* is considered a central aspect of governance, both in the public and private sphere, such as controllership or cost accounting .

Advocacy: It is a political practice carried out by an individual, organization or pressure group , within the institutions of the political system, in order to influence the formulation of policies and the allocation of public resources . Advocacy may include numerous activities, such as campaigns through the press, promotion of public events, commissioning and publication of studies, research and documents to serve their goals. The Lobby is an advocacy so held by the direct approach of the legislators to defend certain goal, and plays an important role in modern politics. Studies have explored the way in which advocacy groups use the media to promote civil mobilization and collective action in defense of particular interests.

Social Capital: It refers to goodwill, friendship, solidarity, social interaction between individuals and families who make up a social unit. If a person barely exists socially if left to himself/herself; but if he or she comes into contact with neighbors, and they with other neighbors, there will be an accumulation of social capital. This would immediately meet their social needs and may bear a social potentiality sufficient to the substantial community improvement and its living conditions. The community as a whole will benefit by the cooperation of all its parts, while the individual will find in his/her associations the help of advantages, solidarity and neighbors at the club. In this sense, social capital is covered in this book.

Citizenship: It is the exercise of civil political and social rights, and duties established in the constitution. Good citizenship implies the interrelation between rights and duties , and the respect and fulfillment of both contribute to a more balanced society. When citizenship is exercised is to be aware of their rights and obligations, and fight for them for further practice. Exercising citizenship is to be in good standing of the constitutional provisions. Preparing citizens for its own exercise   belongs to the country's education goals.

Organizational climate: It is the quality of the environment that is perceived or experienced by the company participants, and such influences their behavior. It is that "psychological atmosphere" that we all realize when we enter a certain environment, and the one that makes us feel more or less comfortable to stay, interact and perform.

Organizational Communication: It is the type or process of communication that occurs in the context of organization , whether public or private. Knowledge and the study of stakeholders of an institution (public), planning of communication practices in the *internal* areas (internal communication) and *external* (external communication) are part of the Organizational Communication. In it the choice and use of executed means, implementation and continuous evaluation is understood.

Public Communication: It relates to the interaction and information flow related to issues of collective interest. The field of public communication includes all matters pertaining to the State apparatus, government actions, political parties, third sector and, in certain circumstances, to private actions. The existence of public resources or public interest characterizes the need to meet the requirements of public communication.

Organizational culture: All customs and traditions organizations (public, private or third sector) have and alter their progress in a positive or negative way, and may be changed over time. Organizational culture involves artifacts (behavior patterns), shared values (beliefs), and assumptions (values, truths). It may also contain visible components, which are always guided by the organizational aspects, or hidden components which are always guided by emotion and affective situations.

Deliberation: It is the action or effect to deliberate or discuss themselves. It is to argue over a controversial subject or debate; discussion whose purpose is to solve a problem. It is a performed act or resolution taken after reflection.

Democracy: It is a political system in which all eligible citizens equally participate - directly or through elected representatives - in the proposal, development and creation of laws , exercising the power to rule by universal suffrage . It encompasses social, economic and cultural conditions for the free and equal exercise of political self-determination.

Deliberative democracy: It maintains that the exercise of citizenship extends beyond mere participation in the electoral process, requiring a more direct participation of individuals in the field of public sphere in a continuous process of discussion and reflective critique of social norms and values. Social and collective issues should be subject to assessment of all, considering that in a democratic society the public sphere (whether physical or virtual) is dominated by discourse and argumentation.

Empowerment: It is the collective action undertaken by individuals when they participate in privileged spaces of decision and social awareness of social rights. This awareness goes beyond the decision of the individual initiative of knowledge and improvement of the reality in which he or she is involved.

Private sphere: It is the opposite and the complement of the public sphere. The private sphere is a particular sector of life in society in which an individual enjoys certain degree of authority, free from government intervention or other institutions. Family and home are examples of private sphere.

Public sphere: It is characterized by forum for debate among individuals in the population; a sphere that begins to be created with the emergence of the press and the application of typography. This was something provided by historic and remarkable invention of Johannes Gutenberg , and by doing so it allowed greater access to information by the general audience. Its strengthening occurs from the nineteenth century, when the newspaper goes on to express the reality in its essence more openly as well as transparently .

First Sector: It refers to the public sector, i.e. the State or Government.

Environmental Responsibility: It is the responsibility that a company or organization has with society and the environment beyond legal and economic obligations .

Second Sector: Represented by the market , which is private .Also known as the productive sector.

Stakeholder: It is a person or a group that legitimizes the actions of an organization and that has a direct or indirect role in its management and results. It is formed by company employees, executives, managers, owners, suppliers, competitors, NGOs, customers, the State, creditors, unions and several other persons or companies that are related to a particular action or project.

Sustainability: It can be defined as the ability of human beings to interact with the world, preserving the environment not to compromise the natural resources of future generations. The sustainability concept is complex because it meets a set of interdependent variables, but we can say that it must have the ability to integrate social, energy, economic and environmental issues.

Third Sector: It includes private initiatives of public utility originated from civil society . It is the set of entities of civil society with public non-profit goals, maintained by the emphasis on voluntarily participation in non-governmental environment.

REFERENCES

Appolinario, F. Dictionary of Scientific Methodology: A Guide for the production of scientific knowledge. São Paulo, Atlas, 2009.

Bardin, L. Analysis of content. Lisbon, Issues 70, 1979.

BRANDÃO, EP Concept of Public Communication. In: DUARTE, J. (ed.) Public Communication: State, Market, Society and Public Interest. São Paulo, Atlas, 2007.

CAPPELLE, MCA; MELO, MC OL; Goncalves, CA Content Analysis and Discourse Analysis in Social Sciences. Magazine UFLA - Rural Organizations & Agribusiness. V. 5, n. 1, 2003.

CORELLA, MAR La Comunicación y en las public private organizaciones. In: Organicom - Journal of Organizational Communications and Public Relations. Year 3, No. 4, [1st.]Half of 2006.APPOLINÁRIO, F. Dicionário de Metodologia Científica: um guia para a produção do conhecimento científico. São Paulo, Atlas, 2009.

BARDIN, L. Análise de conteúdo. Lisboa, Edições 70, 1979.

BRANDÃO, E. P. Conceito de Comunicação Pública. In: DUARTE, J. (org.) Comunicação Pública: Estado, Mercado, Sociedade e Interesse Público. São Paulo, Atlas, 2007.

CAPPELLE, M.C. A.; MELO, M. C. de O. L.; GONÇALVES, C. A. Análise de Conteúdo e Análise de Discurso nas Ciências Sociais. Revista da UFLA – Organizações Rurais & Agroindustriais. V. 5, n. 1, 2003.

CORELLA, M. A. R. La Comunicación en las organizaciones privadas y públicas. In: Organicom - Revista Brasileira de Comunicação Organizacional e Relações Públicas. Ano 3, número 4, 1º. Semestre de 2006.

DEUSDARÁ, B.; ROCHA, D. Análise de Conteúdo e Análise de Discurso: aproximações e afastamentos na (re)construção de uma trajetória. ALEA, v. 7, número 2, julho – dezembro 2005, p. 305 – 322.

DUARTE, J. (org.). Comunicação Pública. Estado, Mercado, Sociedade e Interesse Público. Atlas, São Paulo, 2007.

ESTEVES , J. P. "Espaço Público político" (cap. 1) em Espaço público e democracia: comunicação, processo de sentido e identidade social. São Leopoldo, Unisinos, 2003.

FEIGELMAN, D. B. Valores compartilhados: o desafio de levar a teoria à prática. In: Organicom – Revista Brasileira de Comunicação Organizacional e Relações Públicas. Ano 5, número 8, 1º.semestre 2008.

FREITAS, H. M. R.; CUNHA JR., M. V. M.; MOSCAROLA, J. Aplicação de sistemas de software para auxílio na análise de conteúdo. Revista de Administração da USP, 32(3), 97-109.

GOMES, W.; MAIA, R. C. M. Comunicação e Democracia. Problemas e perspectivas. São Paulo, Paulus, 2008.

_____. Esfera pública política e comunicação em mudança estrutural da esfera pública de Jurgen Habermas .In: GOMES, W.; MAIA, R. C. M. Comunicação e Democracia. Problemas e perspectivas. São Paulo, Paulus, 2008.

GUGLIANO, A. A. Democracia, participação e deliberação: Contribuições ao debate sobre possíveis transformações na esfera democrática. Porto Alegre, Civitas, no. 2, Jul-Dez, 2004.

Guia Exame de Sustentabilidade. Editora Abril, São Paulo, 2010.

Guia Exame de Sustentabilidade. Editora Abril, São Paulo, 2011.

Guia Exame de Sustentabilidade. Editora Abril, São Paulo, 2012.

Guia Exame de Sustentabilidade. Editora Abril, São Paulo, 2013.

HABERMAS, J. Direito e Democracia.: entre facticidade e validade. Rio de Janeiro, Tempo Brasileiro, vol.II, 1997.

HASWANI, M. F. Comunicação pública 360 graus e a garantia de direitos. In: KUNSCH. M. M. K. Comunicação Pública, Sociedade e Cidadania. 1ª. Ed., São Caetano do Sul, SP, Difusão Editora, 2011.

_____. O jornalismo disseminador de informações de serviços públicos governamentais no Brasil: colaboração ou desvio? In: CONGRESS OF THE LATIN AMERICAN STUDIES ASSOCIATION, Rio de Janiro, junho de 2009. Disponível em http://lasa.international.pitt. edu/members/congress-papers/lasa2009/files/WaswaniMariangela.pdf. Acesso em fev.2014.

KIM, J., WYATT, R. O.; KATZ, E. Notícia, Conversação, Opinião e Participação: o papel da conversação na democracia deliberativa. Tradução Carolina Khodr, Juliana Pronunciati e Priscila Souza (2008).

KRIPPENDORFF, K. Metodologia de análisis de contenido. Barcelona, Paidós, 1990.

KUNSCH, M. M. K. (org.). Comunicação Organizacional: histórico, fundamentos e processos. Vol. I. São Paulo, Saraiva, 2009.

_____ (org.). Comunicação Pública, Sociedade e Cidadania. São Caetano do Sul, Difusão Editora, 2011.

LIMA, M. E. A. T. Análise do discurso e/ou análise de conteúdo. Psicologia em Revista, Belo Horizonte, v. 9, n.13, p 77, jun. 2003.

LÓPEZ, J. C. J. *Advocacy*: uma estratégia de comunicação pública. In: KUNSCH, M. M. K. Comunicação Pública, Sociedade e Cidadania. 1ª. ed. São Caetano do Sul, SP, Difusão Editora, 2011.

MAIA, R. Visibilidade midiática e deliberação pública. In: GOMES, W.; MAIA, R. C. M. Comunicação e Democracia. Problemas e perspectivas. São Paulo, Paulus, 2008.

MANSBRIDGE, J. A conversação cotidiana no sistema deliberativo. In: MARQUES, A. C. S. (organização e tradução). A deliberação pública e suas dimensões sociais políticas e comunicativas: textos fundamentais, Belo Horizonte: Autêntica Editora, 2009.

MARQUES, A. C. S. (organização e tradução). A deliberação pública e suas dimensões sociais políticas e comunicativas: textos fundamentais, Belo Horizonte: Autêntica Editora, 2009.

MARQUES, Angela C. S. "Os meios de comunicação na esfera pública: novas perspectivas para as articulações entre diferentes arenas e atores. Em Revista Líbero, Ano XI n. 21, junho de 2008.

MATOS, H. A comunicação pública na perspectiva da teoria do reconhecimento. In: KUNSCH. M. M. K. Comunicação Pública, Sociedade e Cidadania. 1ª. Ed., São Caetano do Sul, SP, Difusão Editora, 2011.

_____. Capital Social e Comunicação: interfaces e articulações, São Paulo: Summus editorial, 2009.

_____.Comunicação pública, esfera pública e capital social. In: DUARTE, J. (org) Comunicação Pública. Estado, mercado, sociedade e interesse público. São Paulo, Atlas, 2007, 2aEd.

MINAYO, M. C. de S. O desafio do conhecimento: pesquisa qualitativa em saúde. 7ª. Ed. São Paulo, Hucitec, 2000.

OLIVEIRA, M. J. C. Comunicação Organizacional e Comunicação Pública. In: MATOS, H. (org.) Comunicação Pública: Interlocuções, interlocutores e Perspectivas. São Pulo, ECA/USP, 2013.

_____.De públicos para cidadãos: reflexão sobre relacionamentos estratégicos. In: FARIAS, L. A. (org.) Relações Públicas: Técnicas, conceitos e instrumentos. São Paulo, Summus, 2011.

Organicom – Revista Brasileira de Comunicação Organizacional e Relações Públicas. Ano 5, número 8, 1º.semestre 2008.

Organicom - Revista Brasileira de Comunicação Organizacional e Relações Públicas. Ano 3, número 4, 1º. Semestre de 2006.

PUTNAM, R. D. Comunidade e Democracia: a experiência da Itália moderna. Rio de Janeiro, Fundação Getuúlio Vargas, 1997.

REIS, B. P. W. Capital Social e Confiança: Questões de teoria e método. Revista Sociologia Política, 21, p. 35-49, nov. 2003.

ROLANDO, S. A dinâmica evolutiva da comunicação pública. In: In: KUNSCH. M. M. K. Comunicação Pública, Sociedade e Cidadania. 1ª. Ed., São Caetano do Sul, SP, Difusão Editora, 2011.

ROSSO, G. e SILVESTRIN, C. B. Comunicação Pública como prática de responsabilidade social das organizações públicas – Organicom – Ano 10 – número 18, 2013.

SANTOS, B. de S. e AVRITZER, L. Para ampliar o cânone democrático. In: SANTOS, B. de S. (Org.). Democratizar a Democracia. Os caminhos da democracia participativa. Rio de Janeiro, Civilização Brasileira, 2002.

SENNETT, R. Respeito: A formação do caráter em um mundo desigual. Rio de Janeiro, Record, 2004.

STEINER, J. The Foundations of Deliberative Democracy Empirical Research and Normative Implications. Cambridge, 20.

STOLLE, D; ROCHON, T. R. Are All Associations A like? Member Diversity, Associational Type, and the Creation of Social Capital. In: EDWARDS, B., FOLEY, M. W.; DIANI, M (eds.). Beyond Tocqueville: Civil Society and the Social Capital Debate in Comparative Perspective. Hanover, NH: University Press of New England, 2001.

STRELOW, A. Reflexões sobre método de pesquisa em jornalismo e uma proposta oriunda do campo. Capítulo 9 in BRAGA, J. L.; LOPES, M. I. V.; MARTINO, L. C. Pesquisa Empírica em Comunicação. São Paulo, Paulus, 2010. (Coleção Comunicação) Livro Compôs.

VALE, G. M. V.; AMÂNCIO, R.; LAURIA, M. C. P. Capital Social e suas Implicações para o Estudo das Organizações. O&S, v. 13, no. 36, Janeiro/Março, 2006.

http://exame.abril.com.br/noticia/itau-unibanco-e-a-empresa-sustentavel-de-2013/imprimir

APPENDIX A

SURVEY OF CASES AWARDED BY EXAMEN AND ABERJE SUSTAINABILITY GUIDES, ISSUES 2010, 2011, 2012 AND 2013

COMPANY	YEAR	RANKING	STATUS	CASE	PROJECT	SECTOR	PAST AWARDS	AGENCY
ALCOA	2010	GUIA EXAME	SUSTAINABLE COMPANY OF THE YEAR	JURUTI	Transform Jurutu to a reference for the sector	Steel and metallurgy	2001,2002	
AMANCO	2010	GUIA EXAME	MODEL-COMPANY	GREEN FORMULA	Alternative Technology investments for the product reformulation	Construction	2007,2008, 2009	
ANGLO AMERICAN	2010	GUIA EXAME	MODEL-COMPANY	COMMUNITARY EXCHANGE FORUM	Community participation in investment proposal discussions	Metallurgy	2008, 2009	
BRADESCO	2010	GUIA EXAME	MODEL-COMPANY	POPULAR RESIENCIAL INSURANCE	Low cost popular insurance. Launched at Morro Dona Marta (RJ)	Finance	2008, 2009	
BRASKEM	2010	GUIA EXAME	MODEL-COMPANY	GROWING UP TO BE GREEN	Research investment for the raw material production and grand opening of the first factory called "green plastic"	Chemical and petrochemical	2007	
BUNGE	2010	GUIA EXAME	MODEL-COMPANY	SUSTAINABLE PACKAGE	Investment on Eco friendly packages	Consumer Goods	2009	
CPFL	2010	GUIA EXAME	MODEL-COMPANY	MARC AND WIND FOR THE FUTURE	Thermoelectric investments moved by biomass of sugar cane and wind parks	Energy	2002,2003,2004, 2006, 2007, 2008, 2009	

COMPANY	YEAR	RANKING	STATUS	CASE	PROJECT	SECTOR	PAST AWARDS	AGENCY
EDP	2010	GUIA EXAME	MODEL-COM-PANY	COME ELECTRIC CAR	Technological improvement and energy fueling posts opening	Energy	2008 , 2009	
FIBRIA	2010	GUIA EXAME	MODEL-COM-PANY	GETING ALONG WITH THE NEIGHBOR-HOOD	Income generation programs to improve relations with the community of its 252 factory locations	Paper and Cellulose	2009	
HSBC	2010	GUIA EXAME	MODEL-COM-PANY	THE INFORMA-TION BUSINESS	Employee training programs forming enviroment leaders	Finance		
ITAÚ BAN-CO	2010	GUIA EXAME	MODEL-COM-PANY	COLLABORA-TION POWER	Employee stimulus for the participation of collective creation for sustainable iniciatives	Finance	2004, 2007, 2008, 2009	
MASISA	2010	GUIA EXAME	MODEL-COM-PANY	MORE WITH LESS	Employees present suggestions to reduce production process inputs.	Construc-tion	2008, 2009	
NATURA	2010	GUIA EXAME	MODEL-COM-PANY	PARTNERSHIPS WITH COMMUNI-TIES	Supplier relations improvement in the whole country to guarantee biodiversity maintance.	Consumer Goods	2000, 2001, 2002, 2003, 2005, 2007, 2008, 2009	

COMPANY	YEAR	RANKING	STATUS	CASE	PROJECT	SECTOR	PAST AWARDS	AGENCY
PHILIPS	2010	GUIA EXAME	MODEL-COMPANY	LIGHT OVER THE PROBLEM	Investment on the production line energy efficiency for the genration of a consumer economy	Electronics	2003, 2005, 2007, 2008, 2009	
PROMON	2010	GUIA EXAME	MODEL-COMPANY	PENCIL POINT BUSINESSES	Sustainability-meter: An index to measure the social-enviroment impact of its projects	Services	2006, 2007, 2008, 2009	
SATANDER	2010	GUIA EXAME	MODEL-COMPANY	HOW TO SPREAD THE RECIPE	Sharing good sustainability practices with clients	Finance		
SUZANO	2010	GUIA EXAME	MODEL-COMPANY	ONE STEP AHEAD	Total emissions impact calculation. Starting from supplies up to the customer.	Paper and Cellulose	2004, 2005, 2006, 2007, 2008, 2009	
UNILEVER	2010	GUIA EXAME	MODEL-COMPANY	GETTING IN-VOLVED WITH TRADITION	Composition alteration in one of the primary products. Eliminating harmful substances for the enviroment.	Consumer Goods	2004, 2005, 2007	
WALMART	2010	GUIA EXAME	MODEL-COMPANY	THE RETAIL FORCE	Stimulate suppliers to rethink their process towards more sustainable processes	Retail	2008, 2009	

COMPANY	YEAR	RANKING	STATUS	CASE	PROJECT	SECTOR	PAST AWARDS	AGENCY
WHIRPOOL	2010	GUIA EXAME	MODEL-COMPANY	RESPONSIBLE TECHNOLOGY	Production innovation avoiding harmful materials, obtaining gains and economic resources	Electronics		
UNILEVER	2011	GUIA EXAME	SUSTAINABLE COMPANY OF THE YEAR	SCALE MAKES A DIFFERENCE	Sustainability as part of the business, influencing 2 billions customers to adopt these practices in their consumption	Consumer Goods	2004, 2005, 2007, 2010	
ALCOA	2011	GUIA EXAME	MODEL-COMPANY	TAKING DIALOGUE SERIOUSLY	Create the sustainable plan after listening the Juruti community in Pará, to become a reference in the sector	Steel and metallurgy	2001, 2002, 2010	
ANGLO AMERICAN	2011	GUIA EXAME	MODEL-COMPANY	PRESERVATION OF ROOTS	Wildlife mapping in the Goiania cerrado. Transforming knowledge into teaching material for the local community	Mining	2008, 2009, 2010	
APERAM	2011	GUIA EXAME	MODEL-COMPANY	STEEL, GREENER AND SUSTAINABLE	Transition from mineral coal to vegetal. Reducing steel production costs and emissions	Steel and metallurgy	2003, 2004, 2007	

COMPANY	YEAR	RANKING	STATUS	CASE	PROJECT	SECTOR	PAST AWARDS	AGENCY
ERASKEM	2011	GUIA EXAME	MODEL-COMPANY	GREEN PLASTIC REVOLUTION	Opening of a new factory of green polyethylene in Rio Grande do Sul and new renewable plastic projects	Chemical and petrochemical	2007, 2010	
BUNGE	2011	GUIA EXAME	MODEL-COMPANY	THE END OF COLD-BUOYS	Labor conditions improvements for the sugar cane cutter and demanding the same from providers	Agrobusiness	2009,2010	
DOW	2011	GUIA EXAME	MODEL-COMPANY	EMPTY BAG FOR STANDING	New package that facilitates recycling and transportation	Chemical and petrochemical	2002	
EDP	2011	GUIA EXAME	MODEL-COMPANY	SMART ELECTRIC NETWORK	Development of an energy meter that allows the monitoring of the consumption in real time.	Energy	2008,2009,2010	
ELEKTRO	2011	GUIA EXAME	MODEL-COMPANY	15 MINUTES POSTS REPLACEMENT	Investment on a state of the art technology and team to increase customer service	Energy	2005, 2006, 2007, 2008	
EMBRACO	2011	GUIA EXAME	MODEL-COMPANY	MORE REFRIGERATION, LESS EXPENSES	Constant investments on research to reduce energy consumption on their main product	Electronics	2006	

COMPANY	YEAR	RANKING	STATUS	CASE	PROJECT	SECTOR	PAST AWARDS	AGENCY
FIBRIA	2011	GUIA EXAME	MODEL-COMPANY	FIGHTING THE GREEN DESERT	Stimulus to the food production. From honey to manioc	Paper and Cellulose	2009,2010	
FLEURY	2011	GUIA EXAME	MODEL-COMPANY	SUSTAINABLE ADQUISITIONS	Brands unification for the classes B and C into a new network committed with sustainable practices	Services		
ITAÚ BANCO	2011	GUIA EXAME	MODEL-COMPANY	STOP FORCING INSURANCES	Product selling changes, more honesty with customers and incorporating sustainability into the business	Finance	2004, 2007, 2008, 2009, 2010	
KIMBERLY-CLARK	2011	GUIA EXAME	MODEL-COMPANY	SUSTAINABLE CRITERIA	Enviorement impact analysis when choosing the new place for next factory	Consumer Goods		
MASISA	2011	GUIA EXAME	MODEL-COMPANY	CLEAN ENERGY CHAMPION	100% renewable energy in the wood panels production process	Construction	2008, 2009, 2010	
AMANCO	2011	GUIA EXAME	MODEL-COMPANY	AGAINST THE LABOR SHUT DOWN	Investment on worker training for the use of their products, increasing their income and company branding	Construction	2007, 2008, 2009, 2010	

COMPANY	YEAR	RANKING	STATUS	CASE	PROJECT	SECTOR	PAST AWARDS	AGENCY
NATURA	2011	GUIA EXAME	MODEL-COM-PANY	THE DO MORE OBSESSION	Adoption of a 100% recyclable package, reducing emissions scrap	Consumer Goods	2000, 2001, 2002, 2003, 2004, 2005, 2007, 2008, 2009, 2010	
PHILIPS	2011	GUIA EXAME	MODEL-COM-PANY	WITH THE HAND ON THE TRASH	Incentives to customers to give back old equipments	Electronics	2003, 2005, 2007, 2008, 2009, 2010	
PROMON	2011	GUIA EXAME	MODEL-COM-PANY	THE GREEN BET	Adquisition of three environmental companies. Getting ready for the green projects era.	Construc-tion	2006, 2007, 2008, 2009, 2010	
SUZANO	2011	GUIA EXAME	MODEL-COM-PANY	ADVICE, PLEASE	Creation of an external permanent group of advisors	Paper and Cellulose	2004, 2005, 2006, 2007, 2008, 2009, 2010	
SABIN	2011	GUIA EXAME	MODEL-COM-PANY	FAMILY IS GROW-ING	Expand the laboratories network withour losing quality service	Services		
ANGLO AMERICAN	2012	GUIA EXAME	SUSTAINABLE COMPANY OF THE YEAR	GOOD NEIGH-BORHOOD POLICY	Dialogue establishment with the communities where it acts. Reducing the environmental impact	Mining	2008, 2009, 2010, 2011	

COMPANY	YEAR	RANKING	STATUS	CASE	PROJECT	SECTOR	PAST AWARDS	AGENCY
AES	2012	GUIA EXAME	MODEL-COM-PANY	SECURITY FOCUS	Investments in public-ity to educate con-sumers. Reducing fatal accidents with electric energy	Energy	2008, 2009	
ALCOA	2012	GUIA EXAME	MODEL-COM-PANY	FOR CLEANER AIR	Change from fuel oil to natural gas, reducing emissions	Steel and metallurgy	2001,2002, 2010, 2011	
BRASKEM	2012	GUIA EXAME	MODEL-COM-PANY	CONSISTENT PROGRESS	8/9 environment index improvements in the last 10 years	Chemical and petro-chemical	2007, 2010,2011	
BUNGE	2012	GUIA EXAME	MODEL-COM-PANY	THE ENERGY FIELD	Renewable energy pro-duction and investment on training for agricul-tural suppliers, reducing emissions	Agrobusi-ness	2009, 2010, 2011	
CPFL	2012	GUIA EXAME	MODEL-COM-PANY	WATER, WIND, SUN	Investment on energy sources. Main bet is on a wind park	Energy	2002, 2003, 2004, 2007, 2008, 2009, 2010	
DOW	2012	GUIA EXAME	MODEL-COM-PANY	IDEAS THAT AVENGE	Partnerships with other companies, seeking for new sustainable business	Chemical and petro-chemical	2002, 2011	
ECORODO-VIAS	2012	GUIA EXAME	MODEL-COM-PANY	ECO ASPHALT	Use of old tires for asphalt construction in their roads	Services		

COMPANY	YEAR	RANKING	STATUS	CASE	PROJECT	SECTOR	PAST AWARDS	AGENCY
ELEKTRO	2012	GUIA EXAME	MODEL-COMPANY	FROM EARTH TO THE AIR	Air inspection to detect network failures to obtain environmental gains	Energy	2005, 2006, 2007, 2008, 2011	
EMBRACO	2012	GUIA EXAME	MODEL-COMPANY	SHARED PROFITS	Suppliers' process analysis to identify potential improvements and distribute gains.	Electronics	2006, 2011	
FIBRIA	2012	GUIA EXAME	MODEL-COMPANY	DOING MORE WITH LESS	Progress in the environment and social areas, despite the poor economic performance	Paper and Cellulose	2009, 2010, 2011	
FLEURY	2012	GUIA EXAME	MODEL-COMPANY	SPEAKING THE SAME LANGUAGE	Strong expansion and new adquisions demand the application of good practices in harmony.	Services	2011	
ITAÚ BANCO	2012	GUIA EXAME	MODEL-COMPANY	STAYING BLUE	Financial education expansion to customers take more responsible actions	Finance	2004, 2007, 2008, 2009, 2010, 2011	
KIMBERLY-CLARK	2012	GUIA EXAME	MODEL-COMPANY	GREEN PACKAGES	Renewable plastic to condition toilet paper. 60% of their product must have sustainable characteristics	Consumer Goods	2011	

COMPANY	YEAR	RANKING	STATUS	CASE	PROJECT	SECTOR	PAST AWARDS	AGENCY
MASISA	2012	GUIA EXAME	MODEL-COM-PANY	DO WHAT I DO	Reduction on the use of a harmful substances in the manufacturing process, guiding the path for the industry	Construc-tion	2008,2009, 2010, 2011	
NATURA	2012	GUIA EXAME	MODEL-COM-PANY	FEET IN THE AMAZON	Creation of an innovation center in Manaus to increase relations with local suppliers	Consumer Goods	2000, 2001, 2002, 2003, 2004, 2005, 2007, 2008, 2009, 2010, 2011	
O BOT-ICÁRIO	2012	GUIA EXAME	MODEL-COM-PANY	GOOD MULTI-PLIER	Incentives to franchises, suppliers and consumers to engage sustainable practices	Services		
PROMON	2012	GUIA EXAME	MODEL-COM-PANY	ISSUE OF PRINCI-PLES	Refuse clients who are not in line with environmental practices	Construc-tion	2006, 2007, 2008, 2009, 2010, 2011	
UNILEVER	2012	GUIA EXAME	MODEL-COM-PANY	HEALTH AT THE GONDOLAS	Reduction of sodium, sugar and other substances in products	Consumer Goods	2004, 2005, 2007, 2010, 2011	
WHIRPOOL	2012	GUIA EXAME	MODEL-COM-PANY	DOMESTIC ECONOMY	Besides water and energy reduction in factories, the challenge is to create products that will reduce cost for consumers	Electronics	2010	

COMPANY	YEAR	RANKING	STATUS	CASE	PROJECT	SECTOR	PAST AWARDS	AGENCY
SABIN	2012	GUIA EXAME	MODEL-COM-PANY	IT'S ALL FOR SOCIETY	Employee well-being policies	Services	2011	
ITAÚ BAN-CO	2013	GUIA EXAME	SUSTAINABLE COMPANY OF THE YEAR		Analysts identified in their reports which companies implies less environmental and labor risks to their investors	Financial Institutions		
BUNGE	2013	GUIA EXAME	MODEL-COM-PANY		Biodiesel plant opening at Nova Mutum, MG, as a clean energy alternative and generating jobs for 10,000 small farmers	Agrobusiness		
TETRA PAK	2013	GUIA EXAME	MODEL-COM-PANY		31% recycling of its own packages. In social area, the company invest in the training of recycling cooperatives	Capital goods		
NATURA	2013	GUIA EXAME	MODEL-COM-PANY		Opening an industrial complex in Pará in 2014 for the exchange of raw material between companies that consider those raw materials disposable	Consumer Goods		

COMPANY	YEAR	RANKING	STATUS	CASE	PROJECT	SECTOR	PAST AWARDS	AGENCY
EVEN	2013	GUIA EXAME	MODEL-COMPANY		Besides sustainable construction inside their apartments, they also include solutions that reduce water and energy consumption	Civil construction		
PROMON	2013	GUIA EXAME	MODEL-COMPANY		Implemented an on-work effluent treatment system in the petro-chemical complex of Petrobras. Saving water	Consulting		
WHIRPOOL	2013	GUIA EXAME	MODEL-COMPANY		The business unit in Santa Catarina, as the biggest refrigerator factory in the world, is transforming its wastes into other materials	Electronics		
ELEKTRO	2013	GUIA EXAME	MODEL-COMPANY		Created a training center for distribution installers and technicians. Since 2008 400 people have graduated and 350 have been hired-	Energy		

COMPANY	YEAR	RANKING	STATUS	CASE	PROJECT	SECTOR	PAST AWARDS	AGENCY
EUROFAR-MA	2013	GUIA EXAME	MODEL-COM-PANY		Established a partnership with Pão de Açucar to collect in their drugstores drugs packages and bottles. Since 2012 it has collected 4.5 tons of waste	Pharmaceutical		
CCR	2013	GUIA EXAME	MODEL-COM-PANY		Created a plan of 7 battlefronts: road safety, education, wastes,mobility, health, food safety, green infrastructure and local entrepreneurship.	Infrastructure		
ERASKEM	2013	GUIA EXAME	MODEL-COM-PANY		Creation of new material that reduces the shoe industry impact. This material helps to skip a process stage that harms the ozone layer	Chemical		

COMPANY	YEAR	RANKING	STATUS	CASE	PROJECT	SECTOR	PAST AWARDS	AGENCY
DURATEX	2013	GUIA EXAME	MODEL-COMPANY		Substitution of Oil Diesel for eucalyptus scraps that are not used in the board of wood production. It also changed oil diesel generators that were old for more efficient ones.	Construction Materials		Lápis Raro
VOTO-RANTIM METAIS	2013	GUIA EXAME	MODEL-COMPANY		It developed reduction and re-use projects of industrial wastes, generating profits.	Mining		
FIERIA	2013	GUIA EXAME	MODEL-COMPANY		To reduce conflicts with the community, the company heavily invested in its social column. In 2012, R$27 million were invested in income generator, life improvement, wood robbery reduction programs	Paper and Cellulose		Cajá- Communication Agency
LAB FLU-ERY	2013	GUIA EXAME	MODEL-COMPANY		The goal is to share the green awareness in the sector, donating time and knowledge from their employees.	Services and Healthcare		

COMPANY	YEAR	RANKING	STATUS	CASE	PROJECT	SECTOR	PAST AWARDS	AGENCY
ALCOA	2013	GUIA EXAME	MODEL-COM-PANY		Through remelting, the recycled material can be re used in the aluminum production or in civil construction. The company, in addition, made focused efforts to reduce its energy consumption.	Steel and metallurgy		Rede comunicação de resultados
ALGAR TELECOM	2013	GUIA EXAME	MODEL-COM-PANY		Since 2011, the Ox in the Line project recycles public phones plastic covers (contains fiberglass) for the use of water container in other industries	Telecommunications		
ECOFRO-TAS	2013	GUIA EXAME	MODEL-COM-PANY		Teach clients about using of a more efficient fuel, despite being a little bit more expensive, the importance of preventive maintance and driving safely brings great benefits to them.	Transportation		

COMPANY	YEAR	RANKING	STATUS	CASE	PROJECT	SECTOR	PAST AWARDS	AGENCY
WALMART	2013	GUIA EXAME	MODEL-COMPANY		Walmart is cleaning its beef suppliers monitoring them and their farms as well. This improves the quality and certifies thse safety of beef according to international standars. They also collaborate with Amazon communities in beef production motivating a sustainable production with NGOs help.	Retail		
SABIN	2013	GUIA EXAME	MODEL-COMPANY		The company supports laboratories from Universities and private researchers with the condition that their employees participate in the projects. The project has received international recognition.	PME		
UNILEVER	2013	GUIA EXAME	MODEL-COMPANY		In 2010, the company shared its objective of doubling its size and reducing by half the environmental impact of its process until 2020	Human Rights		

COMPANY	YEAR	RANKING	STATUS	CASE	PROJECT	SECTOR	PAST AWARDS	AGENCY
NOVARTIS	2013	GUIA EXAME	MODEL-COMPANY		The corporative board is formed by 6 women and 6 men from different nationalities and educational backgrounds. The diversity is even included in their calendar which fits according to the religions each person practices.	Communities		
EMBRACO	2013	GUIA EXAME	MODEL-COMPANY		20 years ago the company started efforts to promote a green awareness among local schools in Joinville. Now the project has expanded to one thousand neighboring private schools. The 700 hundred projects have benefited more than 100,000 people	Suppliers		

114

COMPANY	YEAR	RANKING	STATUS	CASE	PROJECT	SECTOR	PAST AWARDS	AGENCY
ALCOA	2013	GUIA EXAME	MODEL-COMPANY		In 2010 the Sustainable Purchases program was created which is a selection process of suppliers. The company promotes good and sustainable practices and process within their business to suppliers.	Water management		
COCA-CO-LA	2013	GUIA EXAME	MODEL-COMPANY		The company has reduced its water consumption as raw material to create beverages. Now it uses 24% less water.	Biodiveristy		
APERAM	2013	GUIA EXAME	MODEL-COMPANY		In 1993 the company created a Environmental Education center at Timóteo, Minas Gerais, where its plant is. 20 years later the area transformed to become a wildlife reserve benefiting local indigenous communities.	Waste management		

COMPANY	YEAR	RANKING	STATUS	CASE	PROJECT	SECTOR	PAST AWARDS	AGENCY
KIMBER-LY-CLARK	2013	GUIA EXAME	MODEL-COM-PANY		Since 2012, the company has partnerships with local cooperatives to collect and recycle raw materials that can be used in their disposable diaper process. They also transform non-contaminated hospital materials into toys.			Santo de Casa En-domarketing
UN-IMED-BH	2010	ABERJE	Marketing Communication Campaign	Unimed Company solution				OZ Propaganda
COELCE	2010	ABERJE	Communication Enterprise Sustaintability Programs	Ecoelce				Datamidia DraftFCB
SHELL BRASIL	2010	ABERJE	Brand Communication	Partnership between Shell Brasiul and Ferarri at Grand Prize Brasil F1 2009				S/A Comunicação

116

COMPANY	YEAR	RANKING	STATUS	CASE	PROJECT	SECTOR	PAST AWARDS	AGENCY
COELCE	2010	ABERJE	Communication of Programs, Projects, and Cultural Actions	Cine Coelce				Artevento; Burson-Masteller, Expomus, Objeto Sim, Sofia Carvalhosa and Young&Rubican
FIAT AUTOMÓVEIS	2010	ABERJE	Communication of Programs, Projects, and Cultural Actions	Rodin and Chall at the cultural Fiat house				La casa Comunicação
AACD	2010	ABERJE	Integrated Communication	2009 Telethon				Satori Editorial
Secretaria da Sáude de São Paulo	2010	ABERJE	Communication in Company Crisis	Guiding the national action against the flu AH1N1				Grifo Design
COELCE	2010	ABERJE	Relations and Communication with the Press	One foot on the road project				Conspiração Filmes
BUNGE	2010	ABERJE	Relations and Communication with the Society	Know to sustain: Itajaí Valley				

COMPANY	YEAR	RANKING	STATUS	CASE	PROJECT	SECTOR	PAST AWARDS	AGENCY
BRASIL FOODS	2010	ABERJE	Relations and Communication with Suppliers	Club "do produtor de leite Brasil Foods"				
GRUPO VATORAN-TIM	2010	ABERJE	Relations and Communication with Investors	From "no profile" to qualified dialogue				FSB Com-munications
UNIMED LONDRINA	2010	ABERJE	Relations and Communication with Investors	One school for life				
ITAÚ BAN-CO	2010	ABERJE	Relations and Communication with Internal Audience	Itaín Unibanco Fusion				
Secretaria Municipal de Espoertes, Lazer e Rec-reação	2010	ABERJE	Special Events	Virada Esportiva				
Fundação Telefonica	2010	ABERJE	Historic Respons-ability and Com-pany Memories	Exhibition " Tão longe, Taõ perto"				

COMPANY	YEAR	RANKING	STATUS	CASE	PROJECT	SECTOR	PAST AWARDS	AGENCY
PETRO-BRAS	2010	ABERJE	Historic Responsability and Company Memories	Henrique Lange Refinery: A 30 year Adventure				Textual Corporativa; Tatil Design de Ideiais;-Conspiração filmes; SR-COM;Five
AMANCO	2010	ABERJE	Printed Media	Aqua Vitae Magazine				Âgencia Ark,Co-municação; Caramin-holas Produção e Serviços Artísticos
INSTITUTO EUVALDO LODI	2010	ABERJE	Special Publica-tion	Intelectual Property for Industrial Inno-vation Program				
PETRO-BRAS	2010	ABERJE	Audiovisual Media	The Pré-Sal Conquer				LFCom co-municação
PETRO-BRAS	2010	ABERJE	Audiovisual Media	Cultural tag Petro-bras				
Federeação das Industrias do Estado do Paraná	2010	ABERJE	Digital Media	Digital communi-cation of the FIEP system				TIF

COMPANY	YEAR	RANKING	STATUS	CASE	PROJECT	SECTOR	PAST AWARDS	AGENCY
Governo do Estado do Rio de Janeiro	2010	ABERJE	Social Media	GovRJ: Dialogues with the 2.0 citizen				Rock comunicação; Brasil 1; F/ Nazca
HOSPITAL DA BALEIA	2010	ABERJE	Relations and Communication- Small and Medium Organizations	VIII Baleia friends dinner				Report comunicação; ModernSign
HOSPITAL DA BALEIA	2010	ABERJE	Media- Small and Medium Organizations	Baleia newsletter				Noir assesoria; Universo produção; Trendix
ITAÚ BANCO	2010	ABERJE	Enterprise Communication-Company of the Year					Temple Comunicação; Gamma comunicação
COLÉGIOS MARISTAS	2011	ABERJE	Marketing Communication Campaign	Loyalty and endorsement campaing of Colegios Maristas				
Comite organizador dos Jogos Olimpicos e Paraolimpicos Rio 2016	2011	ABERJE	Brand Communication	Brand release for the Olimpic Games 2016				New Quality eventos and Marketing Promocional

COMPANY	YEAR	RANKING	STATUS	CASE	PROJECT	SECTOR	PAST AWARDS	AGENCY
Fundação São Francisco Xavier	2011	ABERJE	Special Publication	"Atitude rima com Saúde"				Fundação Patrimônio Historico de Energia e Saneamento
Província Marista Brasil Centro Sul	2011	ABERJE	Special Publication	Terms, expressions and institutional values guidelines				Maga Multimidia
AYMARÁ EDUCAÇÃO	2011	ABERJE	Printed Media	Ayamará cities: Educational City program relations magazine				
COELCE	2011	ABERJE	Relations and Communication with Society	Social energy				Amyris; Basf; BP; Dedini; FMC; Itaú;Monsato; Syngenta; ALCOPAR; BioSul; SIAMIG; SIFAEG; SIN-DACOOL/MT; OR-PLANA and CEISE BR

COMPANY	YEAR	RANKING	STATUS	CASE	PROJECT	SECTOR	PAST AWARDS	AGENCY
Federeação das Industrias do Estado do Paraná	2011	ABERJE	Relations and Communication with Society	2030 cities				Conteúdo Communicação Empresarial
PETROBRAS	2011	ABERJE	Communication of Enterprise Sustainability Programs	Brazil Surf Pro sustaintability				
NATURA	2011	ABERJE	Relations and Communication with Investors	Communication of Results				Agência Guaimbê
PETROBRAS	2011	ABERJE	Programs, Projects and Cultural Actions Communication	Petrobras celebrates 500 sponsored films				Agência Click
VALE	2011	ABERJE	Programs, Projects and Cultural Actions Communication	Vale music Youth orchestra				Colmeia
Fundação Chesf de Assistencia e Seguridade social	2011	ABERJE	Relations and Communication with Internal Audience	The "zum–zumzum" will start				In Press Porter Novelli

COMPANY	YEAR	RANKING	STATUS	CASE	PROJECT	SECTOR	PAST AWARDS	AGENCY
PETRO-BRAS	2011	ABERJE	Relations and Communication with Internal Audience	The knowledge colors				Populos Co-municação
COMPAN-HIA DE GAS DE SÃO PAULO	2011	ABERJE	Historic Respons-ability and Com-pany Memories	Gas memories- leg-acy to the service of education				
COMPAN-HIA DE HI-DROELÉC-TRICAS DE SÃO FRAN-CISCO	2011	ABERJE	Internal Audiovi-sual Media	Pro genre equality program				
COELCE	2011	ABERJE	External Audiovi-sual Media	Itvea/Midia.com				REPORT COMUNI-CAÇÃO
UNICA- União da agroindustria Canaviera do SP	2011	ABERJE	Integrated Com-munication	AGORA project-Agroenergy and environment				Textual Corporativa; Tatil Design de Ideiais;-Conspiração filmes; SRCOM

COMPANY	YEAR	RANKING	STATUS	CASE	PROJECT	SECTOR	PAST AWARDS	AGENCY
ITAÚ BAN-CO	2011	ABERJE	Communication in Companies Crisis	"Mamaço Itaú Cultural"				EKO ESTRATÉ-GIAS EM COMUNI-CAÇÃO
ASSO-CIAÇÃO PARANESE DE CULTU-RA	2011	ABERJE	Relations and Communication with the Press	PUCPR: A Pa-ranaense univeristy that conquer the national press				
INSTITUTO CAMARGO CORRÊA	2011	ABERJE	Special Events	Good works day				CDN-CORPO-RATIVE COMMU-NICATION
PETRO-BRAS	2011	ABERJE	Digital Media	Biomaps Petrobras				OZ Londria
PETRO-BRAS	2011	ABERJE	Digital Media	Petrobras compact: The petrobras music videocast				Happy hour Brasil
Consessão Metroviária do Rio de Janeiro	2011	ABERJE	Social Media	Metrô Rio in the social network				

COMPANY	YEAR	RANKING	STATUS	CASE	PROJECT	SECTOR	PAST AWARDS	AGENCY
HOSPITAL DA BALEIA	2011	ABERJE	Relations and Communication-Small and Medium Organizations	Be a smiles doctor: Social movement for a Radiotherapy Center construction at the hospital				Grupo maquina PR
Associação Brasileira de Ontopsicologia da Região Sul	2011	ABERJE	Tribute- Media-Small and Medium Organizations	Performance Lider Magazine				Quadrante design
UNICA-União da agroindustria Canaviera do SP	2011	ABERJE	Enterprise Communication-Company of the Year					Memória & Indentidade
NATURA	2012	ABERJE	Marketing Communication Campaign	Plant no Cinema				Vídeos Barrinhas
Comite organizador dos Jogos Olimpicos e Paraolimpicos Rio 2016	2012	ABERJE	Brand Communication	Brand realase for the Olimpic Games 2016				Report Comunicação
PARAGOMINAS MUNICIPAL CITY HALL	2012	ABERJE	Communication of Enterprise Sustainability Programs	Paragominas: from black list to the green list				Plan B

COMPANY	YEAR	RANKING	STATUS	CASE	PROJECT	SECTOR	PAST AWARDS	AGENCY
CASA FIAT DE CULTURA	2012	ABERJE	Communication of Programs, Projects, and Cultural Actions	Italia Brazil moment: Roma, de Chirico e Caravaggio na casa Fiat de cultura				Rede Comunicação de Resultado
KINROSS BRASIL MINERAÇÃO	2012	ABERJE	Relations and Communication with the Press	Global Enterprise, local action: Relations strategies with the local press				FSB Comunicação
UNIMED LONDRINA	2012	ABERJE	Relations and Communication the Society	Water, soa and awareness campaign				Tempo & Memória; Arte do Tempo
BRASKEM	2012	ABERJE	Relations and Communication with Internal Audience	Plastic valuation				
ALGAR TELECOM	2012	ABERJE	Relations and Communication with Consumers	CTBC answers				
BRASIL FOODS	2012	ABERJE	Integrated Communication	Perdigão/sadia Merge judgement				
VALE	2012	ABERJE	Special Events	Botanical Park exhibition				
TICKET SERVIÇOS	2012	ABERJE	Historic Responsability and Company Memories	How to implement a company memories project				

COMPANY	YEAR	RANKING	STATUS	CASE	PROJECT	SECTOR	PAST AWARDS	AGENCY
AMPLA ENERGIA E SERVIÇOS	2012	ABERJE	Audiovisual Media					
NATURA	2012	ABERJE	Digital Media	Natura campus program				
PETRO-BRAS	2012	ABERJE	Digital Media	Future careers program website				
SE-BRAE-MG	2012	ABERJE	Printed Media	Step by step success				
Governo do Estado do Rio de Janeiro	2012	ABERJE	Social Media	#CHOQUEDEPAZ				
SOCIE-DADE BRA-SILEIRA DE DERMATO-LOGIA	2012	ABERJE	Special Publication	Family Bounds: Brazil's ethnicity				
BRASKEM	2012	ABERJE	Enterprise Communication - Company of the Year					
LIGHT	2012	ABERJE	Marketing Communication Campaign	Central Innovative ideas				

COMPANY	YEAR	RANKING	STATUS	CASE	PROJECT	SECTOR	PAST AWARDS	AGENCY
RAÍZEN	2012	ABERJE	Marketing Communication Campaign	Shell V-Power bat-mobile promotion				
CNC	2012	ABERJE	Brand Communication	New brands CNC-SESC-SENACCNC				
FIBRIA CELULOSE	2013	ABERJE	Communication of Enterprise Sustaintability Programs	Fibria Courage stories				
BANCO DO BRASIL	2013	ABERJE	Communication of Programs, Projects, and Cultural Actions	Impressionism Exhibition: Paris and modernity				
VALE	2013	ABERJE	Communication of Programs, Projects, and Cultural Actions	Sponsors set for São Luis 400 years				
CNDL/SPC BRASIL	2013	ABERJE	Relations and Communication with the Press	Information that generates trust and opens opportunities				
ENDESA BRASIL	2013	ABERJE	Relations and Communication the Society	Conscious vote campaign				
ITAÚ BAN-CO	2013	ABERJE	Relations and Communication with Internal Audience	Financial education at Itau Unibanco - Challenges that start with associates				

COMPANY	YEAR	RANKING	STATUS	CASE	PROJECT	SECTOR	PAST AWARDS	AGENCY
GRUPO MARISTA	2013	ABERJE	Relations and Communication with Consumers	#serirmaomarista				
USIMINAS	2013	ABERJE	Integrated Communication	USIMINAS 50 yeats of actions				
OAS INVESTIMENTOS	2013	ABERJE	Communication and Events Organization	Grêmio arena inauguration				
CPFL ENERGIA	2013	ABERJE	Historic Responsability and Company Memories	CPFL, 100 years project				
SULAMÉRICA	2013	ABERJE	Audiovisual Media	Anual report: Friendly language and innovation in accountabilty				
USIMINAS	2013	ABERJE	Digital Media	Internet speaking Usiminas				
PFIZER	2013	ABERJE	Printed Media	Bulletin Include				
IVECO	2013	ABERJE	Social Media	Libertadores 2012				
SINDILOJAS PORTO ALEGRE	2013	ABERJE	Special Publication	Porto Alegre at window shopping- Retail stores Memories				
ITAÚ BANCO	2013	ABERJE	Enterprise Communication-Company of the year					

APPENDIX B Article Guia Exame de 6/11/2013

Itaú Unibanco is the sustainable company 2013-Business

2/4/2014

EXAME.COM

 ## Itaú Unibanco is the sustainable company 2013

Largest private bank in the country with 15 million account holders, Itaú has added the best practices that make it a leader among financial institutions.

Itaú Unibanco was elected the Sustainable Company of the Year by Guia EXAME 2013 Sustainability, which hits newsstands on Thursday. Largest private bank in the country with 15 million account holders, Itaú has added the best practices that make it a leader among financial institutions.

In 2004, the bank was the first to voluntarily adhere to a set of environmental rules for lending to its customers, created by the IFC, the financial arm of the World Bank. Following these principles, in 2012, Itaú denied credit for the construction of the Belo Monte Dam and about other 90 companies have also been disapproved due its social and environmental impacts.

Within the company, sustainability management has been translated, increasingly, into governance. Every employee, no matter what level, is learning to play more responsibly their role in this journey. The idea is to bring sustainability to the center of the strategy.

To help this process, Itaú Unibanco holds a sustainability committee of 20 high executives to discuss solutions to problems (how to improve the care of vendors to serve the public, for example) and they also propose differential actions, such as creating a rental program of bicycles in cities.

"Sustainability has to be good for us and for our customers. We understand that we have to extend our action far beyond what is our business," said the president of Itaú Unibanco, Roberto Setúbal, when accepting the award.

In his speech, Setúbal highlighted some initiatives held by the bank. "We have a cultural institute that promotes Brazilian art in particular. We have social programs quite focused on education. We believe in the program of bikes as a way to improve urban mobility. Everything we do involves a number of ways of acknowledgement on how we improve our relationship with people, with society, "he said.

Companies looking to the future

The most sustainable companies in the year were awarded late on Wednesday in Sao Paulo, in a ceremony at the Maria Luisa e Oscar Americano Foundation.

During the event, the superintendent director of Unidade EXAME from the Publishing House April, Cláudia Vassallo, said that the term sustainability has been used too lightly lately and that, in many cases, it goes far away from the fundamental idea of looking today very carefully in the future effects for the next generations.

"Companies that are here today share the belief that the role of business and business leaders goes far beyond the return to shareholders. They rather believe they can achieve this return in a sustainable way" she said. Claudia highlighted that Brazil has greatly improved, but there is still much to be done.

"The Brazil we want for ourselves and our children and grandchildren is a country where every child can thrive with decent education, where basic education is not a privilege, where children do not have to live immersed with the trash up to the neck to pick cans in exchange for some change," she affirmed, referring to the photo of the boy Paulo Henrique which featured in the newspaper Folha de S. Paulo last Tuesday.

http://exame.abril.com.br/noticia/itau-unibanco-e-a-empresa-sustentavel-de-2013/imprimir